WHO CARES ABOUT BLACK BOYS?

Moving from Acknowledgment to Advocacy

Dr. LaSonja Flowers-Ivory

Dedication

To every Black male who has been educated in the pre-kindergarten through twelfth grade public school system and those who are to come. You are smart, important, unique and strong. I join the ranks of many who have fought and are fighting for the quality of education and learning environment you deserve. You have a role in this fight as well. It is a Civil Rights issue.

Acknowledgments

I thank God for leading me in the direction to research this topic, the past and present opportunities to serve in capacities that permit me to positively contribute to the educational experiences of all students, particularly Black males.

To every parent, teacher, custodian, clerk, librarian, principal, church and others who have seen the plight of Black males and provided positive guidance, care, role models and mentors for them. You matter.

A special thanks to the models on the cover and/or in the book: Trelan Harvey and KiAndrew Rufus, my nephews; Mason Freeman, and Ian Holt, a special young man I had the privilege of supporting as a high school administrator. When I asked them to participate in my project, all three agreed with no hesitation. I am grateful.

Table of Contents

Preface

I am the mother of two Black males and a proud educator. I believe that the fulfillment and satisfaction that comes from caringly opening the eyes, ears, minds and hearts of children is unparalleled.

This book is a brief summary of three years of research surrounding the questions: How do African American males perceive and experience school belonging in a suburban high school? How do their perceptions influence academic engagement? The study examined the nature of the achievement gap through interviews with nine African American high school males. The results of the study address how these students have perceived their educational experiences in public schools up through their junior and senior years in high school.

My goal is to present years of documented research related to African American males and education in a reader-friendly format. While most conversations surrounding race, ethnicity and culture are difficult for some to hold, I am hopeful that business organizations and especially schools will begin to see the need for professional development and crucial conversations to assist with implementing effective strategies to address the neglected educational needs of African American males. Additional motivations for writing this book include the following:

- To communicate the findings in a way that adds to the body of knowledge for P-12 educators

- To share information that can be given to students to help them better understand the effects and/or the benefits of school culture as they relate to student achievement

- To communicate to this gender and race of students that their unique needs and challenges are worth exploring and adequately addressing

- To assist others by providing information that will serve as tools to support their efforts to advocate for children.

- To present evidence for the critical need to improve academic achievement and the overall quality of life for African American male high school students.

- To assist schools with developing a culture that systemically addresses the needs of African American male high school students.

Teachers matter. The significance of their roles will be evident throughout the book. Numerous studies (including this one) validate that children demonstrate great intellectual ability when a teacher has great expectations for their intellectual development. The expectation of the teacher combined with a positive relationship with the students has been documented as a perfect combination for engagement and academic achievement.

When it comes to the status of Black boys in school, too often, attention is focused on the things that are beyond the schools' control, such as poverty. However, educators who refuse to use deficit thinking will agree that each teacher has control of the learning environment in which students are educated. The classroom and the school culture can become a place of healing, hope, nurture, ignition and preparation for students, particularly Black boys.

If you are reading this book, I will assume that you are not only interested in acknowledging the disparity that exist, but you are also willing to do your part in moving from awareness to advocacy. I believe that understanding the perceptions of Black males regarding educators, their school experiences and their sense of school belonging can serve as valuable tools for all stakeholders who are willing to create school communities that advocate for their optimal development.

It will become more evident throughout the book that African American males continue to need others who believe in their abilities to be successful learners. Teachers, administrators, counselors and other adults can help reenforce these abilities.

Introduction

The federal program, No Child Left Behind Act of 2001 (NCLB) created federal and state accountabilities for districts and schools in a wide-sweeping effort to increase student achievement. Meeting the needs of all students is now the stated goal of the United States public school system as evidenced through policies developed such as the 2001 No Child Left Behind (NCLB) Act. On December 10, 2015, President Obama signed the Every Student Succeeds Act (ESSA). This federal law requires data on student achievement and graduation rates to be reported as well as action in response to that data. Under ESSA, states and districts are responsible for supporting and improving the quality of low-performing high schools. One main focus is to narrow the achievement gap between races and holding schools accountable for their scores. As a result, increased attention has been given to the disparity in academic achievement between Black students and other subgroups. No longer can race, language, or culture be used as an excuse for the academic failure of students; schools are now required to produce evidence for the first time in the nation's history that students are learning.[1]

The passage of this bill required teachers to meet particular criteria for their educational institution to be identified as "highly qualified." Although the testing data is disaggregated by ethnicity and schools and districts incur penalties for these subgroups' underperformance, the criteria to become highly qualified does not include training to address these underperforming populations, particularly African American students. In short, the achievement gap that exists between African Americans and other subgroups is the largest. The National Assessment of Educational Progress reports that the average eighth grade student of color performs at the same level of academic proficiency as the average fourth grade White student. This disparity is unacceptable! While this statistic is neither new nor a secret, the continuation of this devastating, careless cycle should be considered malpractice on the part of schools that refuse to adequately address this marginalized group in a way that is valuing and validating. Who cares about Black boys?

CHAPTER ONE

WHY BELONGING MATTERS

The significance of a sense of *belonging* in secondary schools has led researchers to argue that young people need schools that are communities of care and support.[1] When care and support are the foundations of a school community, the needs of the students become a priority, which in turn, effect a positive response from the students. When I speak of the word *community*, I am not referring to a geographic location, rather the quality of relationships in an organization, specifically schools. If members do not experience feelings of belonging, safety, and trust in others, then *community* is not present.[2]

The pseudonymous *community* addressed in this book is *geographically* located at Island High School Pseudoname and describes the quality of relationships between African American male students and others, in particular, their teachers. Island High is a suburban high school with an integrated student body numbering over 3,000 students. The terms *African American* and *Black* will be used interchangeably throughout this book to describe an individual of African descent who identifies with the cultural identity of the United States.

Many students from low-income home and minority backgrounds have not traditionally viewed the school community as a place that fosters quality relationships; rather, they are more apt to see the school as a setting for tension, failure and alienation.[3] Many low-income and minority students face obstacles that are well beyond the scope of school influence; therefore, creating a sense of community and belonging must become a part of the focus within the realm of school control. If schools want to positively impact Black boys socially, emotionally and academically, then teachers must begin to see the value of effecting change and making a profound difference in the lives of these important and valuable young people.

Research indicates that in regard to the alienation and resistance some students feel that *identity* is the key issue.[4] Unfortunately, studies indicate that for many students of color, the school room has become a place where their cultural and academic identity is attacked rather than affirmed. From the spelling and pronouncing of their names to the texture of their hair, many Black students have experiences at school that do not promote positive racial identities. This reality is rarely, if ever, addressed in teacher preparation programs. So, how are teachers supposed to learn this vital information about the students they are paid to educate. Identity formation is a normal developmental process that all young people experience; however, developing a positive ethnic-racial identity in school will support the African American student to better navigate racism outside of school.

The perceptions of African American males regarding educators and school belonging can serve as valuable tools for both educators and students to help create school communities that advocate for their optimal development. This group continues to need others who believe in their abilities in order to become successful learners, and they rely on teachers, counselors and other adults to develop, teach and reinforce their abilities.

While the United States has made progress toward social equity, daily life clearly reveals that divisions and barriers still exist, and numerous factors, including socioeconomic status, gender, and ethnicity/race contribute to these divisions and barriers. In the 1954 United States Supreme Court case of *Brown v. Board of Education*, the racial desegregation of public schools was mandated. Despite a federal law deeming it illegal to educate students separately based on race, this practice has continued. Now, Black students are no longer being educated in separate buildings; however, it is undeniable that they continue to be educated differently.

Over fifty years after the passage of *Brown*, many minority students are still being tracked into lower level courses which do not prepare them academically for more rigorous courses. The Department of Education literature on school desegregation clearly documents the fact that many African American students are not provided a quality education.[5] The dropout rates for Black males continues to increase, and studies outline identifiers as early as fourth grade. It is imperative that schools become the change needed for this marginalized group. A direct correlation exists between high school dropouts and incarceration. In other words, schools that continue to do business as usual in relation to African American students, particularly Black males, are systemically perpetuating the school-to-prison pipeline.

Although fifty years have passed, the alarming dropout rate of African American male students has captured the attention of educational leaders. Many of these dropouts also experience high levels of incarceration in state and federal prisons as well as the recidivism of these young lives. President Obama's federal educational reform program, *A Race to the Top*, set aside funding to provide more intervention to help correct some of these situations. However, creating a culturally relevant culture that values and validates all students cannot be mandated by the government alone; this is not a problem even the President can solve. The state has given local school districts the power to create local policies. School districts and schools must decide to create learning environments that not only acknowledge the gaps in achievement and treatment but also become advocates for their advancement by providing effective and appropriate professional development along with a commitment to a paradigm shift as it relates to this marginalized group.

Understanding and acknowledging how African American males cope with and respond to the cultural environment of their school is critical if educators plan to increase academic achievement for this group of students. In gaining an understanding of their school experiences and attitudes that influence how they perceive their schooling and academic pursuits, the leadership at schools can create communities that will actively seek to eliminate barriers to a sense of student belonging.

This understanding can also assist educators with examining their personal biases and perceptions of African Americans, particularly males, and prioritizing caring relationships with these students in order to positively

Understanding and acknowledging, while very important, is only the beginning of the process.

influence their academic engagement. Enough information is available to assist policy makers with initiating school improvements and reform efforts from a more informed perspective. Understanding and acknowledging, while very important, is only the beginning of the process. Educators must move beyond this point in order to effect real change.

THE PROBLEM IN CONTEXT

To meet the rigorous challenges of these federal directives, educators face many challenges. For instance, African American students traditionally have a lower enrollment and academic performance than White students.[6] Although ESSA has assisted in highlighting the critical academic state of the African American student, the gap has actually widened in the past years, and African American students now account for 14.7% of all dropouts, which is nearly twice the rate of White students.[7] According to the California 2006 Standardized Testing and Reporting Program, about 60 percent of White students scored at proficient or above in English/language arts as compared to only 29 percent of African American students. Similarly, in mathematics, about 53 percent of

White students scored proficient or above, compared to only 24 percent of African American students.[8]

My particular research was conducted in California, hence the previous data. Nevertheless, these statistics represent a nationwide problem and the numbers are similar, which is why the President led the federal government to create a law to intervene.

These few statistics among many indicate that not only are African American students achieving at lower levels than White students, but the African American male is also achieving at a much lower level than the African American female.[9] According to Michael Holzman's report on public education and black male students, this within-racial group gender gap is the widest gender gap of any student demographic group.[10] African American male academic identities and school performances are well-documented; however, some factors are instrumentally forming their identities that require a closer examination. In other words, if interventions are only focused on where Black students are failing in school but do not address how schools are failing Black students, this cycle of underachievement will continue to repeat itself.

School performance of African American males shows great disparity when compared to other student populations. National data show a significant difference between African American males and White students in the areas of high school graduation rates as well as college attendance and completion rates, none of which favor African American males.[11] African American males are more likely than White students to be placed in the lowest academic track, to be disciplined in higher numbers, and to be negatively stereotyped by teachers.[12] This group is also over-represented in special education programs and represents the highest percentages of suspensions and expulsions.[13] This is national data. Across the nation, Black students are enduring the same paradigms. What is the problem? Who cares about Black boys?

ACKNOWLEDGING IS SIMPLY NOT ENOUGH

African American males face a persistent crisis, as they are consistently experiencing lower educational attainment than any other gender-race group.[14] Understanding what this group perceives as barriers, bridges and connectors to school belonging is necessary. Being African American and male creates a different set of dynamics; the combination of race and gender seems to constitute a "double jeopardy," which researchers argue creates further barriers to the success of African American males.[15] According to the Education Trust, reform initiatives have targeted African American males, but little evidence indicates that the interventions have resulted in increased academic achievement.[16] Relevant staff development training should take place before initiatives begin. The changes needed to reform educational experiences for Black males (and other minority students) will require commitment on the part of educators.

In an effort to move beyond acknowledging and awareness, my research and this book is designed to assist educators and others with identifying some of the factors that contribute to the sense of school belonging experienced by African American males and how this sense of belonging influences their academic engagement. This information can assist educators with creating effective and appropriate strategies to facilitate that sense of belonging. Understanding some of the barriers to academic engagement will help the teacher, classroom and school community provide African American male students the opportunity to think about, discuss, and identify educational barriers. Thus, the students themselves may be better able to identify areas that they can mediate and be more willing to seek outside help when the solutions cannot be provided by the institution.

This study primarily consisted of nine in-depth interviews with African American male students (the Island 9). These interviews were conducted with students who attended a suburban public high school located in Southern California. Student interviews were transcribed, coded, and analyzed in order to determine veins of similarity among the experiences of different African American male students within Island High School. Attention was given to the sense of belonging the students felt to their school and how their academic engagement was affected. The questions for student interviews focused on the students' experiences both inside and outside of the classroom, their impressions of belonging, their attitudes regarding their relationships with teachers, their perceptions of the importance of education, and their feelings concerning their classroom involvement.

CHAPTER TWO

WHAT WILL EDUCATORS DO WITH THIS TRUTH?

The troubled status of African American males in school and social life has been documented in several studies. Simply reviewing the following statistics reveals the truth of this paradigm:

- In school, African Americans account for 32% of suspensions and 30% of all expulsions, yet they only represent 17% of the total school population.[1]

- When compared to their White counterparts, African American male adolescents are placed in remedial or special education classes at a rate three times higher.[2]

- Only 8.4% are identified and enrolled in gifted and talented classes.[3]

Schools are sending a message to and about African American males that does not convey or indicate that they are valuable and intellectually capable of academic success. This same message is also evident in the advance academic classes. For example, many schools have academic pre-requisites for advanced courses; the prerequisites are not always ability-based, oftentimes, they are performance-based. If, for example, a student does not have *above average* grades (particularly A's and B's), they are not even considered for more rigorous courses—even if they may be interested and have the ability. When Black students notice that few or no Black students are in the more challenging classes, a message is automatically sent that does not foster a sense of community or school belonging. Based on this research, capable Black students will opt out of the opportunity to enroll in advanced classes due to the fear of more alienation.

Furthermore, the African American male has a one-in-four chance of becoming a dropout statistic from high school and has an even worse chance of graduating from college—one-in-twelve.[4] Sadly, African American males account for a mere 3.5% of the total college and university enrollment in the United States.[5] This alarming statistic is only one of several severe consequences of unequal education today because of the strong link between education and income.[6] For example, some of the severe consequences include an increase in dropout rates, unemployment and incarceration, while college enrollment decreases. These factors critically affect the ability of these students to make positive contributions to society. How can they when their economic future depends on their elementary and secondary schooling that is essentially failing them? African American males need an adequate education not only to have successful school experiences but also to lead productive lives. In addition, the students experience an unequal education that excludes them from the most rigorous curriculum available and all the benefits of intellectual development. Hence, Black males also have a dim future outside of school as a result of the quality of their education. African American males' social experiences are equally as dangerous and as troubling as their school experiences.

* African American males lead the nation as both victims and perpetrators in homicides.[7]

* African American males comprise the fastest growing suicide rate.[8]

* African American males are contracting HIV and AIDS at a faster rate than any other group.[9]

The declining enrollment of Black males in higher education, the declining number of Black males who are gainfully employed, and the increasing number of Black males who are at risk of failing school (often leading to increasing numbers in the criminal justice system) has led several authors to refer to the Black male as an "endangered species."[10] African American males are plagued with a plethora of challenges, some of which are not associated with the educational system. Many Blacks and Latinos, for example, are poorly educated, live around a higher concentration of demoralized people in dilapidated and dangerous circumstances and have few prospects for employment."[11] As a result of these unfortunate conditions and challenges, their educational performance is often connected to the hardships they endure within the larger society.[12] The aforementioned factors are obviously out of the realm of school influence; however, schools could increase their efforts in meeting minority students' psychological and emotional need to belong, particularly when it comes to African American males.

Meeting the need to belong will assist schools with meeting additional educational needs. For instance, when students feel that they belong, the possibility for developing caring relationships is much stronger.

According to some researchers, school failure contributes to many negative outcomes for African American males.[13] For example, many students create discipline issues in class simply to avoid the embarrassment of not understanding the material. Other students lose their academic confidence and give up altogether as a result of school failure. Sometimes indulging in drugs and alcohol are byproducts of school failure. Creating a culture that is caring, intentionally inclusive and culturally competent can help decrease school failure for many students.

Teachers and students constitute the primary members of the school community and when there is a disconnect or tension present, the learning environment is negatively impacted. Needless to say, the responsibility of creating the sense of community in schools belongs to the teachers and the schools. Even when teachers are willing to create caring relationships with students, they would benefit from support in the form of specialized training that is culturally relevant.

In my first year of teaching high school, I remember speaking to a Hispanic male about his inappropriate behavior in my classroom. While I was speaking, he kept his head bowed. I demanded that he give me eye contact and verbally expressed my disappointment with him for being disrespectful. Later that day, I was conversing with my assistant principal and explaining my frustration with this student's refusal to make eye contact with me. Dr. Hernandez, who was also Hispanic, explained to me that culturally, the student was showing me respect. In the Hispanic culture, a sign of disrespect is to look authority figures in the eye while being reprimanded. I felt so dreadful! What I had considered a universal sign of respect was actually cultural.

How could I have accurately interpreted this student's response through the lens of my experience? I was forcing my cultural norms and expectations on a student who possessed a different set of cultural norms. The student and I definitely experienced a communication gap that had nothing to do with language. How can this student experience a genuine sense of belonging when I, as the teacher, was unaware and unknowingly dismissed a cultural value? This incident represents one of many examples showing the need for schools to institute appropriate and effective training in order to create a school culture that is inclusive of all students.

It is important to remember that culture also refers to values, attitudes and beliefs. Providing a safe place in schools for discussions addressing the subjects of race, culture and bias will impact teachers' ability to create and foster relationships with students. Allow me to share a personal snapshot of what I mean.

One of my sons was staring out of the window of his first-grade class, watching the kids play. As a result of his inattention, the following dialogue took place:

Teacher: "Alonzo, would you like to go outside and play with the kindergarteners right now?"

Alonzo [with much excitement] "Yes! Can James go with me too?"

This scene ended with Alonzo in the principal's office for disrupting class. I had to explain to the teacher that the culture of my home does not include using rhetorical questions to make a statement. In this incident, my son was not trying to make the class laugh; he was simply and honestly answering her question. Her reference point was the measuring rod for his behavior, and she assigned a negative value to the behavior. She could not understand why Alonzo would answer yes while the class was in the middle of spelling words. My son could not understand why he was in trouble for answering her question truthfully. While this example may seem trivial, the magnitude of the relationship breach between student and teacher is very real.

The need to belong is a basic psychological need. When students do not feel connected to their school and do not feel valued by their teachers, they are being asked to perform cognitive tasks when their basic psychological needs have gone unmet. Students are obviously unaware of this failure; yet the symptoms are present and continue to persist. Research states that belonging is a precondition for engagement. In other words, when students feel that they belong in the class, valued by the teacher, and an important part of the class, they will engage academically. When schools do not understand or accept this fact, they are insisting that academics are more important than the sense of belonging. Unfortunately, schools that fit this description will continue to fail at closing the achievement gap for Black students.

For the purpose of this study, school belonging is referring to an individual's view of whether he or she feels a part of, accepted and valued by, included in, and connected to the school community and culture.

LABELING AND LIMITED AFRICAN AMERICAN MALES

Interestingly, the gap between White and minority students is minimal or nonexistent at the beginning of their schooling; however, by sixth grade this gap has increased by as much as two grade levels.[14] As a result of ineffective interventions, the two-year gap between minority and White students remains, and oftentimes, increases. According to the Department of Education, at grade 8, there was no measurable difference in White/Black or White/Hispanic mathematical scores between 1990 and 2013—twenty-three years of no growth. We are out of time for experimenting! Research-based solutions are available.

Also, curriculum reform efforts that are implemented in many schools are ineffective as they are designed to *fix* the deficiencies of African American male students.[15] That the students are not responding positively to a curriculum that frames their school failure in terms of something being wrong with them is no surprise. Neglecting to investigate how the organization may have failed the students further estranges the students. Sadly, these programs can further marginalize African American males. For example, a stigma is often attached to after-school tutoring, which is often the method of support offered to at-risk students. While other students are involved in extracurricular activities after school, at-risk students are expected to participate in academic interventions.

THE RELATIONSHIP BETWEEN BELONGING AND ACADEMIC ACHIEVEMENT

The construct of belonging derived from Maslow's 1971 hierarchal theory of motivation and personality is based on the pyramid of basic human needs. According to this pyramid, a person theoretically can move to the next step of self-actualization once his needs are satisfied at each level. Maslow's theory is similar to other theories of development in that resolution is contingent on completion of the previous stage.[16] For children to develop a strong sense of belonging or connection during adolescence is extremely important. Generally, when the need to belong is met, academic performance is increased, teacher-student interactions are more positive, and peer relations are more satisfying.[17]

Anyone with an awareness of the previous models, which indicate the importance of addressing psychological and environmental struggles of African American males, realizes that interventions focusing solely on this group continue to identify scholastic and cognitive variables related to educational successes. Drawing from Maslow's hierarchy of needs, targeting scholastic goals without addressing and meeting the basic needs of students, such as the need to belong, will prove ineffective. Consequently, when students do not believe they are valued or connected to a school community, a basic need according to Maslow, being asked to academically succeed after periods of neglect will prove an insurmountable goal.

With this foundation in mind, the policies and practices of schools that serve adolescents should reflect a priority being placed on belonging and connections. In contrast, alienation occurs when a student feels a lack of belonging or connection. As a general rule, when a school has a large percentage of a particular ethnic group, the group that will feel a diminished sense of belonging to the greater school community will be the students in the minority group. A student's sense of belonging can be negatively influenced when he perceives himself to be exceptionally different from the rest of the students. When schools are aware of these dynamics, appropriate and effective measures can be taken to mediate some of the negative effects. Research has proven that one precursor for students' dropping out is a lack of belonging within the greater school community.

The high school completion rates of students who earn high grades and exhibit academic motivation have been associated with a strong sense of belonging.[18] Encouraging and supportive adult mentors (teachers, counselors, and coaches) have positive effects on school attendance, college attendance, and educational aspirations; however, this support often declines as students reach adolescence. As a matter of fact, students who feel alienated and no sense of belonging often exhibit negative behaviors such as cutting class, hostile behavior, and dropping out. Poor psychological adjustment, alienation, anxiety, depression and loneliness are all related to a lack of belongingness.[19] These multiple symptoms oftentimes lead to negative educational outcomes, and unfortunately, academic performance is viewed as being synonymous with academic ability. In actuality, the Black student has as much learning and achievement potential as any other group.

- African American learners account for 26% of students who are retained in first grade in United States public schools.[20]

- In Texas, they account for 15.4%.[21]

- The percentage increases; African American learners represent 38.6% of students retained in grade 3 in United States public schools.[22]

- In Texas, they represent 19.4%.[23]

This retention data is crucial and should inform educational practices. A 2018 study performed by Green determined that students in Texas retained during elementary school are almost three times more likely than their peers to drop out of high school.[24]

Negative educational outcomes are not always a result of the lack of intellect or academic ability. Black students with above-average intelligence have also been reported as dropouts. Several studies indicate that various school-related variables influence students' educational disengagement and underachievement, regardless of their academic ability.[25] Those variables include, but are not limited to, low values placed on academic achievement, the achievement ideology, attitudes toward school, school and classroom climates, and the quality of student-teacher relationships. Schools and districts who are committed to teaching with learning as the direct outcome must embrace the needed paradigm shift required to leave no Black male behind.

Two researchers, Pang and Sablah, surveyed 100 pre-service teachers and 75 in-service teachers who were enrolled in a multicultural course to determine their feelings about teaching African American students. According to their findings, sixty-five percent of in-service teachers reported a belief that African American students could not be reached even by a teacher with good teaching abilities. Furthermore, the study revealed that the surveyed teachers held a strong belief that the African American community is not supportive of education.[26] The teachers, as a group, also believed that the cultural conflict in communication, along with the working class English dialect between home and school, were the main contributing factors for the underachievement of African American students. This perception, though not communicated verbally, does find a way of expression. When a perceived psychological disconnect between teachers, students, and peers is present, student academic performance suffers. In addition, when teachers believe that Black parents are not supportive of education, this will affect the school to home communication and oftentimes the perception of the Black student.

An optimal learning environment is not created when Black males are taught by teachers who believe that the African American community and culture is not supportive of education. Nevertheless, a positive teacher and student connection can counter this negative effect. In other words, if teachers will focus on building relationships with their students, their perceptions of African American community and their working English dialect will become secondary concerns at most. Therefore, a caring relationship between teachers and students is a critical factor for school belonging and academic success.

One group of researchers suggest that the positive, dynamic interactions between students and their social environment results in academic success for the African American male, contending that African American males' perceptions of themselves in a school context impacts their academic success.[27] A strong sense of belonging can obviously result in a decrease in dropout rates and increase in academic engagement. Therefore, an educator's consistent encouragement, coupled with effective professional development, could aid teachers in understanding how crucial their role is when educating African American students, particularly males.

The need to belong is considered a basic human need and is, therefore, critical for development. For schools to meet the needs of African American males in a manner that can result in a stronger sense of belonging and academic engagement, teachers need to accept the magnitude of their role as primary facilitators of the student/teacher relationship. This paradigm shift on the part of schools could increase the opportunities of African American males at becoming academically successful and counter some of the negative elements of society, such as consistent school failure, unemployment and incarceration.

REFRAMING THE ACHIEVEMENT GAP
AS A TREATMENT GAP

Much attention is given to the achievement gap, but a gap in the treatment of African American males also exists within schools.[28] For instance, Zero Tolerance Policies is a harsh term that sends aa strong message which creates a culture that is not favorable for Black males. These policies mandate predetermined punishments and consequences that do not consider the context of the behavior nor extenuating circumstances. At this point, law enforcement is ushered into the equation.

- While African American students represent approximately 15% of the student enrollment in U.S. public schools during 2015-2016, they account for 31% of students who were referred to law enforcement or arrested.[29]

- In Texas, African American students represent approximately 12.7% of the student enrollment in public schools, yet account for 20% of students who were referred to law enforcement or arrested.[30]

A treatment gap definitely exists. The punishments, which resemble verdicts all too closely, are given unapologetically because it's "policy." African American students again are far more likely than other students to be suspended and expelled than other groups. The disparity is well documented.

- While Black boys represent 8% of the students enrolled in public schools, nationally, they overwhelmingly represent 25% of students who were suspended.[31]

- In Texas public schools, black males represent 6% of students enrolled, yet they account for 30% of those who were suspended. Compare this to White male students who represent 14% of students enrolled in U.S. public schools but account for 25% who were suspended.[32]

- In Texas public schools, White males represent 24% of students enrolled and account for 16% of students who were suspended. The rational disparities in suspensions and expulsions are documented in both elementary and secondary levels.[33]

The problems are systemic. The educational system, as we know it, is broken; it is affecting and infecting Black children.

- In the United States, Black children represent 18% of preschool student enrollment, but they account for 48% of students who received more than one day of out of school suspension.[34]

Yes, you read the statistic correctly—preschool age children.

- In Texas, Black students represent 14.9% of the total preschool student enrollment, yet they account for 37.8% of students who received more than one out of school suspension.[35]

Ring the alarm! The school-to-prison pipeline begins in preschool!

Much of the current focus on the achievement gap frames the problem solely as a matter of inferior performance on the part of African American students—not as a matter of inferior treatment on behalf of schools. While several factors outside of school contribute to the plight of the Black male, the public education system has "flagrantly contributed" to the destruction of Black males' aspirations.[35] Educators have been entrusted with the privileged task of educating all students. Schools that continually allow a population of students to be underserved, namely African American males, model what I call *educational neglect.*

Students' racial and socioeconomic backgrounds influence others' perceptions of them as well as the treatment they receive from adults who work with them in schools.[36] I recall an incident when I was called to leave work by the teacher at my sons' school for a parent conference—while he was only in first grade. This situation sounded pretty serious.

When I arrived to the classroom, I was surprised to see the principal present. The atmosphere was very tense, and my six year old was sitting alone on the opposite side of the room from the adults. I took a deep breath and prepared for the worse. I will spare you the preliminary remarks, and there were many. The bottom line was they wanted to express their sincere concern for my son and thought that I should keep him out of school the next day to seek assistance with some form of evaluation. The behavior that had led to my being summoned from work involved my son's inserting a pencil in the pencil sharpener backward—the eraser first. The teacher was deeply distressed by the fact that he laughed when he nearly destroyed the only pencil sharpener in the room.

While this mistake is age-appropriate, the teacher did not see my son's error in this way. Imagine the learning environment he experienced. Needless to say, that was his last day in this particular school.

Many do not understand how adults can view and treat Black boys in such negative ways—even at a very young age. What is less understood is how the perceptions of African American males and the ways they are treated affect their academic achievements. Standardized test scores reveal that many African American male students are academically unsuccessful, and as a result, they are not performing as well as other racial groups. Clearly, barriers exist within schools that are influencing their academic achievement.

The interpretations of African American males' behavior at school and in the public is troubling to many. When Black males violate school rules or even commit minor offenses, the punishment for them is more likely to be severe.[37] Consequently, questions arise as to why being Black and male causes this group to stand out in such "negative and alarming ways"—not only in school but also in society in general.[38] How did this group develop such an alarming presence at school? I wish I had the answer. However, regardless of the source, the staff who view African American males in this light and the African American male students who are subjected to the negative views are likely to be psychologically affected.

Unfortunately, racial and socioeconomic backgrounds of students have a bearing on the way they are treated and perceived by the adults who work with them within schools. Although the main goal of schools is to educate, for many students, learning in an unsafe environment is difficult. Sadly, at some schools, Black males are consistently marginalized and stigmatized, and though they may not be able to articulate the problem, they are certainly affected by their status.

To address the achievement gap of African American males without addressing the treatment gap is to ask students to ignore the historical mistreatment they have received, risk even more mistreatment by participating in class, seek help from an educator who may have low expectations of them, and trust that an education from this same system will somehow change the treatment they receive. African American males can benefit from appropriate, adequate, and sustainable efforts to decrease the achievement gap; however, the efforts should not be random, but research-based.

At a very young age in school, Black males are more likely to be labeled as behavior problems, as less intelligent, and more likely to be punished with severity, even for minor offenses—often without regard for their welfare. Although minor offenses and violations of school rules may be a disruption of school activities, some negative school behaviors are reactions to the treatment African American male students receive. They often experience social oppression and racism and have adopted a "ritualized approach to masculinity," identified within the literature as the "cool pose," that allows them to cope and survive.[39] This disposition that African American males learn to adopt and project at a young age as an emotionless façade is in response to the damaged pride and poor self-confidence that resulted from

African American males' membership in a subjugated group. Although this disposition appears to serve as a defense mechanism and a strategy for coping, it works against them in schools because it is oppositional to academic identification. Conversely, their method of coping creates a vicious cycle, increasing the negative perceptions and treatment they receive.

Oftentimes, the behavior or lack of academic engagement of African American students is mislabeled as a rejection of school and excellence, when in actuality, academic disengagement is oftentimes a defense mechanism exhibited by African American and Latino students brought about by a school's viewing their cultural identity as negative. Like other defense mechanisms, most people are unaware they have developed them, especially school-age students.

Schools fail when the learning environment for Black males is consistently antagonistic, and Black males learn not to trust educators and resist what is offered by those who severely punish them.

The current academic condition of Black males, which has been consistent, has yielded the most persistent low achieving academic gap among subgroups.[40] The indicators of school failures can serve as guides to assist schools in developing strategic and effective methods to serve and reach this population of students. No longer should schools continue to frame their service to minority students, particularly Black males, in a deficit model that implies something is wrong with the students. For example, when addressing attendance, identify elements within the culture that may serve as barriers to students' sense of belonging. Schools have consistently used externally applied stimuli that have been abysmally unsuccessful, and until the need for belonging is met, methods to change behavior will not be effective. The student who does not have his need to belong met by the school would much rather invest his energy in fulfilling this deficiency in other places rather than learning facts and what he perceives as being useless information, such as quadratic equations. The strategy for increasing school attendance and other academic goals should include elements that also increase the student's sense of belonging. Schools must make aggressive, appropriate, and effective efforts to serve African American males, as if they really believe that no child should be left behind.

ENCOURAGING ATHLETICS AT THE EXPENSE OF ACADEMICS

Recognizing the role that teacher perceptions and expectations play in the formations of these identities, especially in adolescence is critical. The quality of relationships that students enjoy with their teachers in specific classes directly affects how students feel about school, their coursework, and their academic identities. As a result, many African American males focus on other strengths and adopt nonacademic goals that appear more attainable such as excelling in sports and music. Oftentimes, these goals are met with school support. Although not explicitly stated, the implicit message is clear that Black males are encouraged to excel in athletics, and many times are not encouraged (with the same momentum) to excel in academic subjects.[41] Therefore, many Black males view their success in sports or music as far more promising than academic pursuits. Many of them do experience success in athletics and are oftentimes acknowledged by peers, staff, and their community for their athletic abilities. Unfortunately, the appreciation and recognition does not carry over into the classroom; as a result, academic engagement, performance, and achievement suffer as a result. Schools also benefit by gaining a competitive reputation, and the vicious cycle continues.

Creating opportunities for students to participate in school activities, including, but not limited to sports, in the earliest grades possible should be a priority for schools. Institutional encouragement should be given in the earliest grades that non-academic participation is recognized. When interventions are created at all levels, strategies to increase overall school participation should be coupled with these academic interventions. A study conducted by D. N. Lloyd indicated a correlation between early school experiences and behavior problems in later years. The study consisted of a collection of third grade information on 788 boys and 744 girls of whom 24.8 percent and 18.5 percent, respectively, eventually left school without graduating. For dropouts and graduates, in terms of course grades, grade retentions, and standardized achievement scores, a significant difference was already evident. The study indicated that students who were involved in school activities had significantly fewer or no behavior problems in school.[42] Since avenues are available for early identification of students at risk of developing negative views about school that will affect their academic engagement and performance, it is critical that appropriate, research-driven strategies are implemented in schools. According to Lloyd's previous research, participation in school activities in early elementary years is one avenue to address the dropout crisis. Schools should be proactive as early as third grade so the level of school failure experienced by African American males may decrease by the time they enter high school. Otherwise, high school graduation and dropout rates along with college enrollment statistics as mentioned previously for African American males will continue. It is important to note that students can participate in school activities without their sense of belonging increasing. In other words, schools should couple involvement in activities along with emphasizing positive teacher/student relationships.

BIASES WITH POTENTIAL TO BECOME BARRIERS

A teachers' inability to recognize intelligence in minority students, particularly, African American males can be indicative of a bias. Unfortunately, the classroom behavior of African American elementary students can be difficult for some teachers to interpret. When teachers are unable to identify *gifted* traits in African American students because their classroom behavior is different, these students are not recommended for Gifted and Talented Education (GATE). In other words, a Black student may possess above average intelligence and may be capable of succeeding in a more academically rigorous course but may be viewed as a behavior problem (according to the standards of the teacher). As a result, the student will remain on the current academic track, despite his or her academic ability. Consequently, the bias now becomes a barrier for the student. In fact, minority students who meet the academic qualifications for GATE are also affected by this bias. For instance, a student referral or nomination from a teacher is the first step in this subjective process. Obviously, a teacher's perception of an African American male student plays a significant role in their academic journey. Research indicates that a teacher's ability to identify gifted students accurately is one of the most important factors affecting students' acceptance into the GATE program.[43] Thus, challenging educational opportunities can be missed, and Black students may not experience their fullest academic potential. Consequently, teachers become barriers to access and serve as "gate keepers" to gifted classrooms for African American students as well.[44] Thus, having teachers who are trained to identify intelligence in African American students as well as identify their own personal racial biases in order to avoid acting as academic barriers to African American males is imperative.

Another example of biases serving as barriers was revealed in several other studies. The researcher, Matthew McBee, conducted a study of 705,074 elementary students in Georgia that indicated teachers were much more likely to refer Asian and White students than their Black or Hispanic peers to GATE programs.[45] When the cultures and behaviors of students are different from the dominant culture and linguistic backgrounds are different, teachers may have negative attitudes about and lowered expectations of these students; thus, these students are often overlooked for rigorous academic programs, such as GATE. Similarly, in a 2005 study, researchers Hala Elhoweris, Kagendo Mutua, Negmeidin O. Alseikh, and Pauline Holloway found race to be a factor regarding teacher referrals to the gifted programs.[46] Some teachers simply believe that African American students do not have the intellectual capability to be academically successful in gifted programs. Clearly, effective staff development programs, along with research-driven conversations with all stakeholders, must become a systemic part of school practices. In regard to addressing the subjectivity of teacher referrals of students to more rigorous courses, including gifted programs, which often overlook African American students, collaboration and accountability, would be critical. Furthermore, this paradigm shift will provide more opportunities and access to students who have been historically denied access to advanced and gifted programs. African American males and their teachers need to know that they are welcomed, academically capable of succeeding and expected in accelerated programs such as GATE.

BEHIND THE SCENE OF DISENGAGEMENT

Several theories regarding self-esteem and identification have been offered in reference to young black males. The effect that feedback has on different individuals depends on the value the individual places on the domain being addressed.[47] Several authors argue that individuals *selectively* devalue domains in which they or their group perform poorly. Therefore, African American males who are underperforming in school may selectively devalue academics and are unaffected by feedback given in this area. In academics, these students are considered *dis-identified*. Dis-identification is a defense mechanism that allows students to disconnect their self-esteem from academic domains and redirect their focus on other areas such as music, sports, and peers.[48] Individuals selectively value domains in which they or their group perform well.[49] Research consistently reveals that African American males are particularly vulnerable and more susceptible to disengagement than any other group. When students are dis-identified with academics, they are neither intrinsically motivated when they perform well nor are they affected by poor performance. This response baffles many educators who initiate conversations with dis-identified students regarding their failing grades. As can be easily seen, Black males have adopted another defense mechanism in order to cope with school experiences. Oftentimes, defense mechanisms are not conscious decisions, they are more subconscious.

Educators generally do not understand the source of disconnect. The apparently careless disposition of the student, which is oftentimes interpreted as a lack of concern, is actually a learned coping mechanism that enables African American male students, in particular, to protect their self-esteem. For instance, if a student is not performing well and the teacher seeks to address the academic symptom alone, the teacher may see a nonchalant attitude and wrongly interpret the student as being apathetic about his education. This teacher's interpretation usually results in consequences for the student or in a strained teacher/student relationship, either of which can cause the student to erect even stronger defenses.

Another element that contributes to African American males' lack of student success is the relationship factor between the minority student and the school. Minority students may regard school as valuable; however, when they are educated in a majority context, oftentimes, the feelings of strong connections or belonging do not develop due to negative experiences with members of the majority group. The academic performance and engagement of African American males, according to researcher Keonya C. Booker, may not always be a result of the value placed on school. Some researchers argue that students of color are prevented from seeing themselves as scholars and oftentimes do not value academics due to factors inherent in American society, such as the limited number of professional, educated, Black male role models.[50] Because dis-identification contributes to or causes poor academic performance, finding and addressing its cause is critical. Teachers and students alike could benefit from understanding this principle along with its repercussions. When teachers understand the causes of dis-identification, they are better able to identify it and become proactive or at least be equipped to respond properly to African American males with the goal of positively and effectively redirecting these students.

Studies indicate that various factors contribute to students' attitudes toward school. The vast majority of Black students, including males, would like to do well in school; however, they are hindered in a variety of ways, including, but not limited to:

- The attitude of students in secondary schools toward academic achievement is often highly influenced by their peer group.[51]

- School practices and curricular issues are crucial factors that affect how African American males process their academic identities.[59] African American males are more likely than White students to be placed in the lowest academic track, to be disciplined in higher numbers and to be negatively stereotyped by teachers. As I have already mentioned, this group is over-represented in special education programs and represents the highest percentages of suspensions and expulsions.

Statistics overwhelmingly reveal that the most highly stigmatized and stereotyped group in American is African American males. Unfortunately, negative forms of treatment in schools are more likely to be directed toward African American males because adults often perceive the behavior of Black children, males specifically, as hostile and insubordinate. Others suggest that Black males have particularly fragile egos and are susceptible to treating even minor slights and transgressions as an affront to their dignity and sense of self-respect.[53] I must wonder how many of these fragile egos are the direct result of the negative forms of treatment young Black men have experienced both inside and outside of school systems.

For African Americans, the lack of academic success can

also be the result of a phenomenon known as the *stereotype threat*, a social-psychological threat that occurs when an individual fears the possibility of fulfilling a negative stereotype. Undoubtedly, all students suffer from some anxiety in school situations, but minority groups experience this anxiety to a higher degree simply because minority stereotypes abound. This stereotype threat can powerfully impact the academic performance of African American students. This fear could cause the student to become self-protective and reduce his identification with academics, thereby fulfilling the stereotype and reducing the anxiety created by the situation.

To demonstrate this point, in a study of college students by Claude M. Steele and Joshua Aronson, cognitive interference was created by telling the students before taking an intellectually challenging test that group differences would be part of the results. By making this announcement, the achievement of stigmatized individuals was suppressed. The two researchers further argued that the knowledge of taking a test designed to show group differences was enough to create a situational stereotype threat.[54]

While NCLB reports test scores document the student group-testing gap, the stated purpose is to eliminate that achievement gap. NCLB's practice in regard to reporting test data racially contradicts Steele and Aronson who suggest that unconscious cognitive interference is created for students when group differences in test scores are emphasized or even noted. For stereotype threats to influence academic engagement in the classroom is possible, especially when there are only a few Black males (oftentimes, only one) in a class. For example, if a Black male is called upon to answer a question in class, his reaction may be a response to the pressure he feels to answer correctly, believing that his response is a direct reflection of his race. This conflicting feeling could set the stage for the dynamics associated with stereotype threat. Evidence of this will appear in quotes from the interview with students in Island High School.

THE IMPACT OF TEACHER EXPECTATIONS ON STUDENT SUCCESS

Education research literature generally states that the social support and encouragement that African American students receive from teachers influences their performance to a large degree more so than any other group.[55] Caring teachers can create a strong foundation for learning, and when teachers challenge, care for, and are interested in educating the whole child, African American students' self-expectations are increased and their belief in their potential to achieve is also heightened.

The Forum for Education and Democracy released data suggesting that the single-most important school influence on student learning is the quality of the teacher. Therefore, to improve access to a quality education and the academic achievement of students attending urban public schools, highly trained teachers are needed. Not only do urban public-school students need highly trained teachers, they also need teachers who are culturally competent. Black students are far more likely to respect and respond to teachers who build and foster positive relationships with them. Students who feel acceptance, connection, and understanding from their teachers are more easily motivated to achieve and work harder to meet their instructors' expectations.

Prudence Carter's research on African American and Latino urban high school students raises an important question about how schools process these students' cultural identities. Her research, for example, suggests that African American and Latino students experience successful engagement and academic achievement when school officials recognize and affirm these students' cultural identities as opposed to perceiving their cultural identities as the basis of their academic underachievement.

For example, I served as the administrator at a high school that employed a White school counselor who was known for telling Hispanic students that watching Spanish television was hurting them academically. He went farther by adding if they wanted to excel in this high-performing school, then they needed to stop watching Spanish television. The counselor was not private about his philosophy, and this known and accepted practice had been occurring for years. Several discussed his attitude with disdain, but nothing was ever done about it. Schools employ other covert ways to imply and verbalize the belief that cultural identities contribute to a lack of academic achievement. What is important to point out is that African American and Latino students and teacher relationships are based on educators' awareness and affirmation of the students' racial identities.[56] Unfortunately, in many schools, little to no emphasis is placed on cultural proficiency in teacher credentialing programs or the average in-service meetings.

MORE BARRIERS TO BELONGING

Since Black males are more likely to be tracked into low-ability courses, they are less likely to receive honors or assigned to advanced placement courses. Black males need opportunities and preparation that will enable them to be successful in more rigorous courses; they also need courses that include culturally relevant content. Research reveals that the lack of culturally affirming curriculum leads to a lower level of academic achievement for minority students.[57] Multicultural curriculum needs to encompass more than the periodic spotlights of people of color that supplement the primary curriculum.[58] True multicultural curriculum is infused throughout with contributions of people of color. Proponents of multicultural curriculum believe that this approach gives people of color a visible presence in academics and will assist with reducing stereotypes and anxiety. The advantage to reading materials that reflect an Afrocentric perspective is that Black students will view their culture as a rich heritage that is filled with a history of educational pursuit.

Some would argue that understanding the cognitive processes that influence how individuals adapt, cope, and respond is the only way to change behavioral outcomes; therefore, understanding attitudes that influence academic pursuits and perceptions of schooling must be part of the beginning efforts to improving the academic performance of African American male students. Underachievement patterns can be reversed when schools are willing to re-evaluate current policies and practices in order to meet the academic needs of African American students. Creating a nurturing condition for academic engagement, coupled with resources and supports, will produce schools where academic success will not be the exception but the norm.

Some of the behaviors of African American male students will be challenging to eradicate because they have become culturally engrained and the result of consistent, systemic school neglect. The literature review on the educational experiences of African American males reveals that more highly qualified, culturally competent teachers, who are sensitive, knowledgeable, and responsive to the educational needs of African American male students from elementary through high school are needed to serve this often-marginalized group of students. These students must be given more academic opportunities in terms of challenging curricula and special programs to build their confidence in their ability to be academically successful while retaining their cultural identity.

CHAPTER THREE

WHEN CARE
IS A VERB

Culture, like pain, is not visible, but is a definite reality and feeling. This study sought to expand the literature by providing a better understanding of what nine African American male students thought about the institutional factors influencing their academic performance. To gain insight into how schools as institutions may enhance or inhibit the educational experience for African American students, the study examined a number of factors that may have impacted the experience of this study's target demographic. These factors included perceptions of relationships with their teachers, their connections to the school, their definition and attitude of academic achievement, the part their culture plays in the learning experience, and the value they place on their membership in their school community. When these factors were perceived as barriers to academic engagement, the influence of these factors on their classroom participation were examined.

The interviews I personally conducted with the Black high school males will provide the reader with a glimpse of how they were influenced by the school culture. Their perspectives are given in direct quotations that have not been edited nor summarized. They are real, and as you take the time to briefly meet these young men through the pages of the book, value their voice and allow them to speak. Failing to recognize the reality of their culture, while easily recognizing long-accepted patterns of culture, only creates invisible pain that is a definite reality. My hope at this point is that all of the research previously presented will become more real, more recognized, and undeniable. I now present the main attractions of the book, the Island 9.

CHAPTER FOUR

MEET "ISLAND 9"

MATTHEW

Matthew was a 17-year-old senior and athlete who did not like school during his freshman year. He had failed English and math in his second term. English was his least favorite class but after developing a relationship with his tenth grade English teacher, he moved from a college preparatory English class to an advanced placement (AP) English class and stated that English was now his favorite class. This student exhibited a strong sense of academic pride, a high level of social awareness, and emotional intelligence. Matthew plans to attend a four-year university and had a career goal in mind.

MARK

Mark was a 16-year-old junior, athlete, and AVID[1] student. He was one of three participants who had never failed a class but admitted that vocabulary and math were his greatest challenges. His favorite class was English because it was his first AP class (required by AVID), and several athletes were in the same class. He planned to attend a four-year university but was undecided about a career goal.

LUKE

Luke, a 17-year-old senior, planned to attend a community college and transfer to a four-year university. His main goal was to graduate from high school and move on with his life.

JOHN

John, a personable 17-year-old senior, was outgoing and appeared to enjoy the opportunity to be heard. John mentioned that his favorite teacher was a Black female, and he stated, "She put up with a lot from me during my freshman year." He felt fortunate to have her as a teacher for a second time and admitted to listening to her more. His future plans included attending a four-year university and majoring in business management.

PAUL

Paul, a 17-year-old senior, was the only student who had previously considered dropping out of school due to home and school difficulties. This student's favorite teacher was a Black male, who he credited for opening his eyes to "a lot of things." For instance, Paul stated that this teacher was responsible for his taking school more seriously and paying attention in class. He mentioned going to a university but was not aware of the requirements.

SILAS

Silas, a 17-year-old senior, had one favorite teacher, a Black female, and stated that she had taught him a lot more than U.S. history; she taught him "how to tell right from wrong." The "A" he received in her class was the first in his high school experience.

TIMOTHY

Timothy, a 17-year-old senior and athlete, attended an academy within the school. This academy, a smaller learning community, offered similar advantages as the AVID program, such as enabling students to take AP classes and helping them understand and meet a-g requirements. Timothy did not have a favorite teacher, but he was one of the few students who had never failed a class. Timothy planned to attend a four-year college.

SAMUEL

Samuel, a 17-year-old junior and athlete, was one of the few students who had never failed a class. He described his relationship with his teachers as "average, nothing special." Samuel had never had a favorite teacher and mentioned that he had always struggled with science. Samuel was considering matriculating to an out-of-state, four-year university.

DAVID

David, a 16-year-old junior, athlete, and AVID student, had a favorite teacher who taught United States history, and he enjoyed learning in her class. History was his favorite subject, and he planned to attend a four-year college, play basketball, and major in history.

MAJOR THEMES

This chapter presents the four major themes that emerged during the investigation based on the two primary research questions:

1) The differences in school belonging experienced by student participants included the differences between athletes and non-athletes. Some students did not feel that they belonged at all; some students felt a sense of belonging because of their peers, while others felt a sense of belonging due to their sports team. The overall school experiences varied for athletes and non-athletes. The athletes were surrounded by adult staff members who served as support, while the non-athletes were not.

2) The majority of student participants who experience academic engagement seemed to be influenced by caring student-teacher relationships. While these students had average to below average grades and participation in other classes, the relationships that were established with caring teachers influenced their class participation, student learning and ultimately academic performance.

3) The majority of the student participants expressed a need for a culturally relevant curriculum. Many of the students voiced feelings of being overlooked by the lack of representation of their culture in the classroom. Participants expressed that an acknowledgment of African Americans' accomplishments would give them something in which to take pride, help to counter the negative stereotypes perpetuated by the media and dispel some of the negative beliefs that some hold regarding the intellect of African Americans.

4) Participants expressed different views regarding the role of race in their academic environment and performance. While some participants expressed neutral feelings regarding their academic environment, stating that it has been their only

experience and therefore, the norm; others expressed a desire for more diversity. Some of the participants also expressed how their race influenced their academic performance.

I noticed a sizable difference in school experiences for athletes and non-athletes. All the athletes socialized in a specific area of the schoolyard that is called the *football bench* by other students as well as by the staff. The high school athletes are provided many additional benefits such as teacher and administrator's recognition, social status, popularity, and academic support. Student athlete participants in this study experienced school belonging directly related to their status and popularity that provided them benefits such as mentors and supports. Conversely, non-athlete student participants were not a part of any school club or student organizations, and their sense of belonging was generally based on satisfaction with social interactions with their peer group.

School belonging for non-athlete student participants seems to be with informal student peer group associations. Unlike the athletes, the non-athlete participants did not share a common group of friends. John, one of the non-athletes, however, did socialize near the football bench. This student enjoyed the popularity that was associated with the athletes who gathered around the football bench.

All students in this study who reported having a favorite teacher experienced an improvement in academic engagement and performance in that teacher's classroom. I did not define the term *favorite teacher*; rather, I asked the students if they had a favorite teacher, and each student defined why a certain teacher was his favorite. Each student's description of his favorite teacher shared a common theme, i.e., a perception of caring on the part of the teacher that resulted in the development of a caring, teacher-student relationship. Each participant was then motivated to participate in class and improve his academic performance. Each participant with a favorite teacher mentioned the above average grade in this class in comparison to the grade in same subject the previous year. The improvement in performance was also reflected in his academic transcript. Most of the participants (five of six) who had a favorite teacher were athletes.

The third theme involved the expressions of the students in this study regarding a desire for a more culturally relevant curriculum and more representation in the Black male student population. This theme was interesting in the sense that it was related to the other themes of belonging to the school in terms as to whom they are as African American students. All the students stated that they believed they would have more friends and receive recognition as a group, if more Black male students attended.

The fourth and final theme addressed how race influenced the academic performance of the participants and their desire for an increase in the Black male student population.

THE STUDENTS' PERCEPTIONS OF SCHOOL BELONGING

This section is the first of three themes to be addressed in this study. In the process of trying to comprehend the experiences that contributed to the participants' feelings of school belonging, three sub-themes emerged:

* Students' Perception of School Connections

* Students' Perceptions of Their School

* The Athlete and Non-athlete Divide

Understanding the perceptions of the participants regarding their school experiences became an important goal of this study. When asked their favorite thing to do in school, all nine participants' responses were essentially the same; they liked to socialize. Likewise, all of them had a consistent area on campus where they assembled during break and lunch. The athletes, regardless of sport, socialized at the football bench. The sense of belonging, for the athlete participants, was not race; it was athletics. The Black athletes reported that they were dispersed among the group, and race did not divide the team. The non-athletes had a specific place on campus where they socialized as well.

The sense of belonging was not defined by race for this group either; rather, their social experiences and the satisfaction they gained from their peer relationships defined their group. Two of the three non-athletes, Luke and Paul, had separate peer groups from each other; however, they both reported that their peer groups were not Black students. The other non-athlete, John, reported his being friendly with many athletes allowed him the privilege of spending time near the football bench. He explained his relationship with the athletes as follows:

Yeah, I hang out at the, well right next to there's a bench with all the football players, the football bench basically and ours is right next to that so you can basically say the tables are like together because we all communicate with each other.

This student enjoyed the shared attention of being near the athletes.

Varying degrees of school belonging became evident among the participants. Some felt a sense of belonging to the school because of their peers or the positive relationships developed through socializing, while others expressed a sense of belonging because of sports. Five of the nine students who, with the help of some teachers, began to develop school belonging through learning and preparing for college and a better future. These students were beginning to experience a shift in their thinking regarding school. For example, Matthew and Mark were taking their first AP or honors class during their junior and senior year. Both Matthew and Mark stated that they had been reluctant to take more rigorous courses in previous years because of the workload, the absence of other Black students, and their perceptions of their academic ability.

When Mark was asked about his knowledge of Honors and AP classes, he responded, "I know that the work is harder, and normally there are no Black people in these classes. That's why we [Black students] don't wanna take them, but since we in AVID, we starting to take these classes too." Seven of the nine participants made statements that AP classes were essentially for the "smart kids," and these same participants did not view themselves as part of the smart group. For example, when describing his teachers, Mark stated, "Some of them are nice, but some of them only like the smart kids."

When Timothy was asked to explain what he knew about AP and Honor classes, he responded, "That they are high, they're advanced classes and usually like intelligent kids or the more smarter kids take them."

Conversely, caring teacher relationships influenced Matthew, Mark, David and Samuel to accept the challenge to take more rigorous courses. Their thinking shifted from a focus on the increased workload to accepting the academic challenges of AP courses.

The participants' sense of school belonging was influenced by what the students valued, what they felt a part of, and what encouraged them to engage academically. Hearing their perceptions about their school setting and other experiences was critical to this study. When asked how connected they felt to their school, four of the nine students reported not feeling connected at all; three of these four were athletes. For instance, Matthew, who was an athlete, stated:

> Unfortunately, not that connected, like football would probably be the main thing that's connected me to school, but other than that, I mean, I come to my classes and I go. Part of that I blame myself; coming into high school, I didn't get into ASB [Associate Student Body] or clubs.

This student expressed a diminished sense of school belonging once practices and games ended. Matthew, like several others in this study, did not have any expectations of the school as a learning institution where belonging is facilitated, nor did they hold the institution responsible for any of their negative school experiences.

Mark expressed a similar response to Matthew's when asked how connected he felt to Island High but took a long pause before replying, "Honestly, not connected at all—like not to the school anyway, but I like playing football." He expressed having a connection with his peers, who were fellow athletes, but he did not know what would help him to feel more connected to the school.

The following student noted his seasonal belonging to the school and blames himself for not finding additional ways to become more connected. Silas reported, "During football season I feel like I'm a big part of the school, but I'm a senior now, and I'm done with football. I feel a part of it [school], but it's not the same." Again, football is the main school-related activity that provides this student with a meaningful sense of belonging to school, and according to his interview responses, football is equated to his peer group.

The one non-athlete participant reported not feeling connected to school and replied, "Well, I guess just for me, school, I've never really felt a deep connection with it." This student had not encountered a teacher who had tried to establish a caring relationship with him nor someone he considered a favorite teacher. Neither was he involved in any clubs or school activities. He was also one of the four who did not have an African American teacher during school. Silas also mentioned that his peer social group at school did not include other Black students. He could not think of anything that his teachers or the principal could do to help him feel more attached to his teachers, the administrators, and/or staff.

Six of the nine students reported feeling that they had a caring teacher relationship. For instance, John proudly expressed, "[I feel] really connected, I know everyone basically, even teachers I don't have I know them somewhat, and they somehow know me." John liked being popular; although he was not an athlete, he spent every day near or visiting the football bench. It was understood that the football bench was for a select group of people, and others were welcomed as visitors only. Timothy declared, "I feel real connected. When I graduate, I want to stay here, not stay in the school but help out." This student expressed that while only one teacher stood out as his favorite, he considered others nice and helpful.

Peer groups created belonging for some participants. Relationships were important to John. He explained, "Well, the reason I feel connected now because, like, I know a lot of people, and I have a lot of friends at my school, so that's the reason why I feel connected." John's identity was tied to the students he knew and the students who knew him. His statements expressed more pride in popularity than academics or anything else school-related. This participant had the lowest grade point average of the nine, while he managed to develop relationships that attracted him to school, he did not experience academic success.

When asked about other social aspects of their school experiences, eight of the nine students expressed a desire for more Black male students. Eight of the participants felt the experience of having more Black male students on campus would be positive. All stated that they would have more friends and be able to relate to more people.

There was no record of racial division among the athletes, and the common interest among this group was clearly sports. The connection was not based on race. The Black male population at Island High was small (less than five percent), and the Black male athlete population was smaller. They had learned how to navigate through a school where the African American student population was less than five percent. This was also true of the non-athletes; two of the three non-athletes stated their peers were not other Black Students. Their peer group connection was also based on something other than race.

THE STUDENTS' PERCEPTIONS OF THEIR SCHOOL

While most of the students expressed positive feelings when asked to describe their school, some admitted having mixed feelings. Two of the nine responses mentioned academics. For example, Matthew pointed out, "it's a good school, concentrated on academics," but he also conceded, "It's also easy to get distracted." Samuel commented on the AVID program and the annual college tours scheduled for grades nine through twelve AVID students. "The AVID program is good, it's what makes me like the school, we go to actual colleges." Still, Timothy had a different perspective and noted that although Island High was a good school, there was "a lot of drama and too many fights." I found it interesting to note that most of the students focused on the positive. Their statements were general without many details.

For example, Luke stated, "It's a good place if you want a out-of-culture experience." This student went on to explain that being Black placed him at a disadvantage because nothing at school resembled anything like his culture. I asked the participants to list one change they would like to see instituted in their school. Five of the nine students did not know what they would change or felt that nothing needed to change. They went on to say that they do not waste time thinking about things being different because it's been like this for so long. Three of the Island 9 listed demographic changes. For instance, one student mentioned changing the way the school is "so sectioned off, so segregated."

Mark elaborated on his desired change, "I would have more Black people here—students and teachers, even office workers. It would just be good to see more Black people. Most of the time they treat you like family and are glad to see you and talk to you."

Paul's comment focused more on the African American student representation at the high school: "I would change the percentages of races. I think I'd try to even it out to 25 percent of each race so everybody could feel comfortable." Some of the participants stated they would have more friends because relating to their own race is easier. Matthew thought that more Black males would bring recognition to their race, stating, "It would force the students and school to recognize us more. I feel like if it was more of us, then principals would have meetings with us and like talk about how to make it our school too."

Timothy shared his perspective on the idea of an increase in Black males. "I think the Mexicans would chill out some because there will be more of us, and I think the school would pay more attention to us too." None of the participants, however, expressed animosity toward their school or any other race. Except for a few participants, the majority of the students could not identify areas in the school or anything about the school that needed to change. Their comments were always about what they personally could do better or what they wish they would have done differently. For example, when asked to identify a grade they would like to repeat, most of the participants stated grade nine. Many mentioned not knowing how important grade nine was until it was too late. There were no references to any favorite teachers or any type of injustice as a reason for this common desire; rather, their reasons were similar in that they did not take high school seriously their freshman year. Six out of nine participants failed at least one class during their freshman year. However, all of them have retaken the courses and are on track for graduation.

What are we doing to prepare them for ninth grade? Too often preparation for ninth grade begins in the eighth grade and rarely is it positive. Some eighth grade teachers speak of high school as the bogeyman: "When you get to high school, their work will be harder, the teachers will be meaner, the schools will be bigger." While, I believe the motive is to create a sense of urgency or awareness, this method of preparation does not work. The preparation to which I am referring is in educating the students about credits and graduation requirements with practical examples and discussions. In my opinion, this conversation should be on the increase by grade six.

THE ATHLETE AND THE NON-ATHLETE DIVIDE

My initial impression was that the student athletes would feel a strong sense of school belonging, but that was not the case for the student athletes who participated in this study. Three of the six student athletes' feelings of belonging were only seasonal; after their sport season was over, they reported their sense of school belonging to be different. Although they experienced a lesser sense of belonging, they still felt they belonged. Two of the athletes were involved in more than one sport, so not having a sport to engender belonging did not present an issue for them. However, for the other four students who played only one sport, the ending of a season had a definite emotional effect on them. They acknowledged that when there were no games to look forward to at the end of the school week and the spotlight of excitement that they once received was redirected to athletes who participated in a different sport, their experiences changed.

Mark expressed his sentiments, "It's different for me because, like, when football is over, I, like, don't have practice, and I have a lot of free time, and it seems like everything is different. Now everybody focus on basketball."

David added, "I should be use to it by now; I'm a senior.

But it's kinda boring at school now, but I don't have to stay up so late to do my homework no more."

For many of the athletes, their identities and motivations centered on the excitement and popularity of being active athletes. Although the experience of the football bench was inclusive of all sports, the conversations were driven by the sport in season. Fortunately, the athletes described the climate of the bench as one of camaraderie more than competition. As athletes, the participants had earned status and popularity, and the supports they received were provided throughout the academic year. Their sense of belonging remained; however, the main adjustment for each of them in terms of school belonging appeared to be personal, individual, and related to feeling a sense of loss in attention and popularity.

Although sports played a major role in the lives of six of the nine participants, relationships were developed with teachers, coaches, and peers that helped the students focus on their academic goals that extended beyond the sport. Athlete participants appeared to use sports as a pathway to navigate through the high school curriculum and move on to a college education. However, this mindset and focus appeared to be the result of the systemic support through athletics. All the athletes reported having a goal of attending a four-year university; however, the non-athletes, who were all seniors, were not only ineligible to attend a four-year university but also did not express a desire to attend one. The athletes voiced the opportunity to play sports after high school encouraged them to apply to college. This implies that schools have missed years of opportunities to capture these students by creating a culture of care and the only experience they want to duplicate is the one created by the positive athletic environment.

One non-athlete, John, self-reported an inflated grade point average and announced that he would be transferring to a four-year university, despite the fact he had not applied to a college or the university after the deadline to apply had passed. Coaches were not required to facilitate the academic safety nets that were provided for the athletes; however, many of the athlete participants would have had different stories if the built-in supports offered to them as athletes did not exist. The information regarding and access given to AP courses is an added benefit of being an athlete.

All athlete participants stated they were enrolled in AVID after making their sport team. According to the athletes, players are expected to be in AVID, unless they are a part of the law academy, which is a program especially designed for students who desire to pursue a career in law. The law academy also has a college focus. Once a student met the requirements to join a sports team, his name was given to a counselor, and, if the student was not in the law academy, AVID was added to his class schedule. This personalized academic attention is valuable in a school where the population of students is over 3,000. In such a large school, students often do not receive such individualized attention.

In contrast, the non-athletes were neither involved in AVID nor encouraged to take more rigorous courses. Based on each of their transcripts, which revealed basic level courses, average to below average grade point averages, and low state test scores, the non-athletes were not academically prepared for more rigorous courses. Yet the athletes were in college preparatory courses with the intention of taking at least one AP course by their senior year. Pointing out that although Matthew, Mark, David and Samuel have an interest in continuing to play sports when they get to college is important to note; however, none of them mentioned receiving an athletic scholarship or becoming a professional athlete.

Athlete participants and coaches alike appeared to view sports as a pathway for students to navigate through high school and onto college. Mark describes some of the academic motivation he received as an athlete: "All the coaches tell us things like, you gotta get good grades to play ball and be in AVID so we can like go to different colleges—not just the ones around the corner."

Timothy speaks of the excitement on game days regarding grade checks: "It's cool to see everybody on Fridays getting their grade sheets signed, but you can tell the ones who not so happy. They don't have theirs in their hands; it's like in their notebook or something."

David shared, "It don't matter to me what college I go to. I'm just glad I had to keep my grades up for basketball, and now I can graduate and go to college, I think, *yeah, all the athletes graduate; that's all they talk about at the football bench now.*"

Athletics at Island High not only offered social benefits but also provided an academic support group for some students.

While it may be true that not all athletes at Island High are taking advantage of the academic supports offered, all athletes in this study were in academic courses that met graduation and NCAA requirements. In addition, four out of the six athletes were in AVID, and one was in a small learning community within the school. The football players were assigned football *buddies*, i.e., a staff member who volunteered to serve as mentor to a football player for one year. If the student and mentor reported that a positive relationship was being developed according to the goals that were established between the student, mentor, and coach, then the match was considered a success and continued another year.

According to the football players, feedback from football buddies was given to coaches each quarter and evaluated by the team of coaches at the end of the year. The basketball players stated that because their team was smaller than the football team, their coaches served as their mentors, and each varsity player was responsible to mentor a junior varsity player. The participants who were varsity players mentioned that junior varsity basketball players were also expected to mentor freshmen. The goal of the team, as stated by David and Samuel, was to have an adult and a peer for support.

In a school this size, the facilitation of relationships that were components of the athletic program at Island High, such as AVID teachers, peer and adult mentors, served as an additional support mechanism. Not only were there academic benefits to playing sports, such as access to AVID, college prep courses, grade checks, and a minimum grade-point-average expectation, but peer and adult role models also helped these

Black male student athletes to successfully complete high school. These were obvious benefits from the guidance given to athletes and the relationships that were formed.

Through sports, it appeared that the participants developed and maintained the discipline they needed to remain academically eligible and take college prep and honors classes. According to the transcripts of each athlete, none of them dropped below a 2.0 grade point average at any point in the school year. In addition, only the athletes in AVID understood the value of AP and honors classes and were taking their first honors and AP classes when they were juniors and seniors, respectively. Yet only three of the six athletes were taking an AP class. The same three of the six athletes had been approached about taking AP classes because taking an AP class is a goal for each AVID student.

In contrast, the non-athletes, who were also seniors, were taking standard-level courses that met graduation requirements only and had never been approached regarding more rigorous coursework. One of these non-athletes had not passed the CAHSEE,[2] which placed him in danger of earning a certificate of completion instead of a high school diploma. For the participants in this study, athletes experienced academic and social benefits that non-athletes did not. The sense of school belonging differed for each participant, and many of them attributed their belonging to their satisfaction with peer group. Overall, the students had positive things to say about their school. There was an obvious gap in the school experiences of athletes and non-athletes. Another aspect of school belonging

STUDENTS' PERCEPTIONS OF THEIR RELATIONSHIPS WITH TEACHERS AND THEIR ACADEMIC ENGAGEMENT

Student-teacher relationships and their performance along with student perceptions of other teachers were two subthemes that emerged from the main theme in this section. The goal of caring teachers is to encourage, motivate, and inspire students to learn, and this study suggests that the participants responded positively when this occurred.

Students will look to find something that they can gravitate to and rely on in order to feel a sense of belonging in the academic environment. When caring relationships were established between teacher and student, students often reciprocated with a strong appreciation of learning. Matthew summed up the importance of this notion when he stated, "There's a lot of great things in the world—money, stuff like that, but there's nothing that compares to when you're in class, and you have the same level of understanding as the teacher on a certain topic." This statement expresses the student's desire for a level of academic achievement that results in personal gratification. Matthew viewed having the same level of understanding as his teacher as a great accomplishment. When asked if they had a favorite teacher, six of nine students replied in the affirmative, and all their answers were relationship-based. The participants also described how they felt about learning in the class. Below are descriptions of the teacher-student relationships from the perspective of the six students who reported having a favorite teacher.

MATTHEW

Matthew was one of the more articulate and thoughtful students when it came to describing his relationship with teachers and how these relationships personally affected him. One of his teachers decided to share something personal about herself at the beginning of the school year before she asked the class to share information about themselves. Matthew considered the initiative taken by this teacher to be an expression of care. This teacher demonstrated a level of transparency that was rare for him: "You could see the scar on her chest, and like, that scar spoke."

For Matthew, this connection with the teacher ran much deeper than the surface scar because this teacher had shared personal experiences from her own life. Her explanation for talking about the scar was to emphasize the importance of perseverance and to encourage her students to respond to challenges in the same way, according to Matthew.

What was of particular interest about Matthew's interactions with this teacher was that the relationship was personal and school-related. As Matthew stated, "She'll talk to you about other things than just school." He also stated that when he sees her on campus, they still share conversations, even though two years have passed since he had taken her class. Not only did

Matthew describe the personal nature of the relationship, he described how this teacher motivated him:

> It was English [the class she taught] and that's not really, I mean, it's probably one of my strongest subjects now, but it's ironic because I don't like it. I didn't like English, but she was my English teacher. She actually helped me turn my whole way of viewing school around because prior to my sophomore year, my freshman year I came into school being lazy, thinking, *I'll have four years at this school. I can take freshman year off.* I could take it easy, so I did, and when I came back sophomore year, she was probably the motivational factor for me about my school life. So, she helped me visualize school in a whole different way and turn my grades around; learning definitely helped me in that class.

This relationship encouraged Matthew to pursue academic excellence in English and challenge himself: "After reading one of my papers in class one day, she called me to her desk, called the AP English teacher on the phone and moved me into English AP herself, then she talked to the counselor." Matthew pointed out that the teacher warned him that the advanced class would be challenging but assured him of his ability to succeed. This episode is an example of a caring teacher who served as a student's academic advocate.

Matthew reported that he enjoyed learning in this class: "She made it fun to learn and when it's fun to learn something, you like to do it. So, I liked learning to write essays." Evidently, the interaction between teacher and student influenced the academic engagement and academic performance. Matthew pointed out, "She actually helped me turn my whole way of viewing school around." This student kept a serious face when describing his relationship with his favorite teacher, but relinquished smiles whenever he talked about his grades or other academic accomplishments in this class. His responses and body language suggested he took pride in this achievement. Somehow, the teacher was able to effectively motivate him not only to engage in the subject matter but also to excel academically.

Matthew identified characteristics in this teacher that were nurturing and caring. He mentioned the teacher's contacting some of his other teachers to receive updates on his academic and behavior progress in their class. According to Matthew, this teacher scheduled a conference with one of his teachers after he received a below-average grade on a test. Matthew reflected, "She was like my school mom."

For instance, Matthew credits his change of attitude toward school and learning to the many talks he had with her and the encouragement he received from her. This teacher offered support, but she also held him accountable by following up on his missing assignments and calling his home when he would "get lazy," according to Matthew. This accountability was not limited to her class alone; she expressed concern about his other classes as well. Matthew earned his first A in English his sophomore year. His experience is an example of success as a motivating factor on its own. He continued to comment on his academic success in this class, "I liked, you know, doing vocab tests and getting back a 19 out of 20 or 20 out of 20. So, when you like to do something like that, you're going to try your hardest." Matthew has maintained an A average in English since his sophomore year and credits this teacher, "I owe it all to her as a teacher."

Prior to his sophomore year with his favorite teacher, Matthew acknowledged that his motivation for performing in class was maintaining his eligibility to play football; he stated that learning was not his goal. The caring relationship he developed with his favorite teacher helped him find value in learning that went beyond the football field.

MARK

Mark reported that the caring relationship with his favorite teacher did not begin with teaching. Mark stated that on the first day of school, this teacher decided to share parts of her life as a mother with the class. To Mark, this transparency set the tone for how he responded to her the rest of the school year: "After that, it was like we family, and she cared about us before she even knew us." Mark mentioned that this was rare and that he felt good about being in this class from the first day. When Mark began to reflect on his favorite teacher, he pointed out:

> She could relate to the athletes; she got two sons who was athletes in high school, and she know how hard it is to be a student and athlete, having long practices, being tired and still doing homework. We do work but not a lot of homework, but that might change [sic] since football is over.

Mark mentioned feeling a sense of belonging with this teacher because she recognized his contribution to the school through sports and that she attended many of the games to support her students in different sports, but football was her favorite. This approval meant a lot to Mark; he interpreted her interest in him as an athlete as sign of her caring. Mark perceived her sensitivity to their football team practice and game schedules as a sign of her concern and was appreciative.

She often made time in class to talk or write about extracurricular activities, and the athletes were encouraged to keep a sports journal. If they chose to share their thoughts with her, she collected them and made comments before returning them. Mark stated that her personal interest made him want to make her proud of him in class. He explained, "She tells me things like, I can do it, and I gotta get prepared for college."

The attention she gave to the students and the meaningful activities that took place outside of the classroom had classroom benefits. According to six of the nine students, the care that was shown by their favorite teachers, regarding their sports and other interests, encouraged them to do their homework and participate in class. These caring teachers appeared to have a relational approach to teaching that created a learning environment. As a result, the participants' self-respect and academic self-image improved. The relational approach provided motivation for academic engagement for participants that resulted in above average grades in that class.

Although Mark struggled with English, his relationship with his favorite teacher positively affected his academic engagement and performance, "I like it [learning in this class]; it's not boring but I struggle with vocabulary 'cuz there was a lot of words that I never heard before." When he discussed his interactions in class, Mark expressed a level of comfort that allowed him to asked questions in this class, although he described himself as shy. However, he reported that he answers questions in other classes "only when the teacher calls on me." This, however, was very different from his interactions in his favorite class.

In an effort to stay on top of his assignments, Mark took advantage of the open-door policy that his teacher had during lunch and after school. As a result, his classroom engagement increased along with his academic performance. Mark was earning a B in the class at the time of the interview. Mark did not appear satisfied with his grade and offered an explanation, "I'm getting a B because I need to study for the tests more, and I can do that now that football season is over." Mark pointed out that the opportunity to get additional help after school is not offered by every teacher. Although this student required additional help outside of the classroom to be successful, he did not interpret the availability of the teacher as part of her assignment.

JOHN

John's favorite teacher was one who also established a caring relationship with him. Although he took a long pause before saying her name, a big smile preceded his words. He mentioned that he had this teacher every year in high school except his junior year. When I asked why she was his favorite teacher, his answers were not related to academics. "She just put up with a lot from my freshman year until now." He expressed gratitude for her patience and "never giving up" on him. He acknowledged that he was a different student his freshman year than he was at the time of the interview. He attributed his attitude toward math to his relationship with his favorite teacher: "I learned a lot, learned everything about math from her."

His freshman year, he failed math; however, he managed to pass math his sophomore year, but his grades were below average. John stated that his teacher was teaching him two years of math during this one year, and he had to work hard to pass the class. He failed math his junior year and is retaking it with his favorite teacher as a senior and is earning a C. John recognized the uniqueness of this teacher: "She does lectures, and she is actually weird, because, you know, a lot of teachers don't have time to explain to each and every individual student if they need help, but she does." He continued to express his amazement by stating, "I don't know how she does it, but she does it, and yeah, so basically everyone in the class is getting something out of it is what it seems like to me."

John has this teacher twice this year, one period for math and the other as a teacher's assistant. He mentioned that he was surprised when the teacher approached him about being her assistant, and he confessed that he thinks the reason is so she can keep an eye on him. This statement was communicated with a big smile. John persevered because of a caring and supporting teacher.

PAUL

Similar to the relationships Matthew, Mark, and John enjoyed with their favorite teachers, Paul's relationship with his favorite teacher was initiated by the teacher. He also spoke with a smile on his face while discussing his favorite teacher. He mentioned the influence of this teacher with conviction. The difference between Paul's favorite teacher and the other favorite teachers was that this teacher was an African American male. According to Paul, the teacher was concerned with his supposed careless attitude and invited Paul to stop by and see him during lunch one day. Paul described the interaction with his teacher by stating, "He's opened my eyes to a lot of things I would never think was true or people wouldn't tell me." Paul interpreted the teacher's actions as caring. He expressed that he was surprised that he and his teacher had similar family experiences.

This personal connection motivated Paul to do better in the class this teacher taught. Paul began to laugh while trying to express his thoughts about the class. "I like learning in this class because it's a lot of fun, but besides a lot of fun it gets serious and you learn more than about just what's in the class." This was not Paul's perspective of the class prior to the lunch conversation with this teacher. Paul began to describe the process of how his perspective about improving his life changed.

He kind of told me his background story, which a lot of teachers don't really tell you. And so learning about him being, you know, in the projects and what not and how it sort of related to me because I was in the projects at one time and how he made it out, it makes you wanna [sic] make it out.

Paul was earning the first A in his high school career; this academic engagement was a by-product of a relationship developed and initiated by a caring teacher who happened to be African American.

The relationship with Paul's favorite teacher was similar to other student participants in the study in that he cared about him personally. However, Paul related to his favorite teacher on the basis of his similar racial experiences, which was critical to influencing his academic engagement and performance. For example, Paul stated that after the lunch meeting with his teacher, he not only felt better about himself but was also motivated to do better in this class. The other participants met their favorite teachers earlier in their high school careers and were able to benefit not only from the relationships but also from the academic impact of those relationships on their school performance.

Paul has experienced a lot of school failure, but one teacher has managed to develop a caring relationship with him that has reinforced his racial identity and influenced his academic attitude and performance. If this student is to be successful, he will need additional support to help him transition from high school and find positive options for his future. This support may come from a local mentoring program or a relationship with a caring adult who can serve as a role model and give him some academic guidance.

SILAS

Silas also described his favorite teacher as one who cared about him as a person. He mentioned several talks before and after class when the teacher addressed several issues, namely, the choices he was making regarding friends. Silas reported that to change his peer group, he began to spend time in tutoring with this teacher after school as this was the time he was spending with the wrong friends. The caring teacher-student relationship that developed as a result of the initiatives taken by this teacher improved his decision-making skills.

When I asked why this teacher was Silas' favorite, he stated, "She's my favorite teacher because she taught me how to stay out of trouble, different paths to succeed." Silas explained further, "She taught me what's right and what's wrong, and like what to do in school and how to motivate me." This student reported spending time with the teacher after school occasionally and reported that the conversations varied from sports, other classes he was taking, college life and sometimes U.S. History, which was the subject she taught him. When asked how he felt about learning in this class, Silas reported, "Well, at first I didn't really care and then she, like, pep talked me, what I have to do to succeed, that's what made me want to change." The student reported becoming more engaged by participating in class discussions, asking and answering questions and learning the material. His final grade in the class was an A.

Like the other four participants, Silas' relationship with a caring teacher yielded academic results, such as increased engagement and academic performance. When asked about his motivation for earning the A, Silas responded, "I think it would have to be her talks." This student had this rich experience his freshman year, and he is the only one of three freshmen who had never failed a class, perhaps, partly due to this relationship with his favorite teacher. This teacher has kept track of Silas by maintaining relationships with his other social science teachers and by having him as her teacher's assistant for one period.

DAVID

David's favorite teacher's teaching approach or style helped David to develop a positive relationship with her. As he put it, "She actually teaches us. She's not mean about it. She actually relates to kids to where like they enjoy learning from her." He mentioned all the different ways that his teacher would teach her subject and the interesting projects that were created during class: "The way the format that she taught us in helped us understand the work, but it also made it fun for us to actually learn the way she was teaching us." David's relationship with his favorite teacher did not appear to be as personal as the others; however, he described her as caring. David described the relationship by stating, "She spent individual time with me a little bit before the last period because I have basketball period, so I had time to learn with her, learn more work." In addition to being academically engaged, his academic performance in social studies improved. The previous year, he earned a D in social studies, but, according to his transcript, he has maintained a B-plus average for the last two years. This was his World Civilization teacher, and now David wants to major in History.

NOTHING COMPARES TO A TEACHER WHO CARES

Of the nine participants, three reported not having a favorite teacher, and they all gave general responses when asked why. Their responses suggested they had not given this question much thought as none of them had a specific reason. Silas stated, "They all teach the same. Like, all the teachers do the same stuff and teach the same way; there's nothing, like, that stands out about them. So how can one be my favorite?"

Another participant revealed, "That's they job to teach; I don't think they wanna be anybody's favorite."

These three young men had very different classroom experiences than the six with a favorite teacher. I think this is important for schools to note in order to build a culture that systemically approaches learning with a relationship framework to increase academic achievement.

In summary, all grades earned in the class of favorite teachers were B or better (3 A's and 3 B's). The results would seem to indicate that caring, nurturing relationships with teachers not only influenced academic performance, but participants stated that there was also an increase in academic engagement. The six students who had favorite teachers reported they increased their classroom participation through asking and answering questions in class. The caring teachers, who were considered favorites, demonstrated their concern in a manner that the students understood. These actions by their favorite teachers were interpreted by the students as caring ones, and the teacher's caring attitude was a consistent theme throughout all of these student-teacher relationships that influenced academic attitude, engagement, and performance. Although not articulated, it was evident that the teachers had high expectations of the participants. The teachers demonstrated caring on two levels: giving the students personal attention and caring about the students' learning. Also, the teachers who were identified as favorite appeared to have a teaching style or teaching approach that resulted in student learning.

In addition to caring about the student as a person and student learning, these teachers apparently had the teaching ability that facilitated student learning, as described by the students. When asked the race of their favorite teacher, the participants identified three of the four teachers as African American.

According to five of the six participants who reported having a favorite teacher, their increased participation in class was reflected in asking and answering questions. John commented on the difference in his relationship with the only Black male teacher. He said this with a big smile and excitement in his voice: "It was definitely different, it was more on a...it was way more on a personal level than a teacher-student level, you know, because he knew a lot of my family so he's like a...I guess you could say like an uncle." Paul had this same teacher for a different class and stated, "We should definitely have more Black teachers at our school, that's for sure, because Mr. Brown is one of my favorite teachers, and I actually learned a lot just about life from him." John, like Paul, received the only A on his transcript from this teacher. Mark commented on the following experience with his Black female teacher:

> I had one Black teacher and that was really cool, she understood me and it was like we was family, she was hard on me but in a way like she talk to me like she was my aunt or something, she thought I was smart and told me I could always do better, but sometimes she accepted my work and just said good job, she was cool, not like my friend or nothing but just a good teacher. I think there should be more Black teachers in our school cuz they understand Black students in a different way than other teachers, yeah, we need more.

STUDENT-TEACHER RELATIONSHIPS AND STUDENT PERFORMANCE

When each of the six students who had a favorite teacher were asked if they had ever failed a class during high school, four of the six students said yes. Six of the nine students had failed a course in the ninth grade. When I asked each student to describe their relationship with the teacher of the course they failed, each of them gave different answers. What they all had in common was the blame they placed on themselves for failing the course—not the teacher. Matthew listed specific personal factors that contributed to his failing grades:

> I failed my algebra class and my English class. I know why it happened. It happened because I failed the term

three and term four and that was after football was over, and we didn't have grade checks anymore. And I really didn't like my English or my Algebra class, so I took it for granted and like thought, *I have three more years, why is my freshman year going to count?* So, I slacked off. I didn't care. That's why I got those F's.

Another student confessed, with a look of disappointment, "I was ditching class." Paul hesitated before giving his explanation for one of the classes he failed:

> Because like I just don't feel comfortable talking to some of my teachers and they don't look like they really wanna talk to me either, so I just show up but like I wouldn't do any work cuz like I didn't understand anything.

The fourth student explained "Math was just something I...it's not one of my greatest subjects. My teacher was a nice lady. She actually took the time to teach us, but I just didn't understand it. She was a good teacher though." According to Samuel, the interactions with this teacher were minimal. By comparison, the students' positive relationships with their favorite teachers seemed to influence their academic engagement and performance.

I asked the students to describe what I would see if I observed them in a class other than the one with their favorite teacher. Their responses were similar. One student explained, "Well, you would see me bored, looking around at the class and probably looking at the clock every five minutes, waiting for the bell to ring." Another student added, "Uh...you would see me sitting there listening to the teacher, bored to death." David responded, "You'll see me probably really quiet and doing my work." Another student mentioned, "You would see me trying really hard just to pay attention and do some work just to stay occupied." The common denominator for all these participants' responses was a lack of interaction with the teacher and student engagement. Their interactions in and attitudes regarding some of their other classes were vastly different from the classes taught by their favorite teachers, where they each experienced the most academic success. Even though the students blame themselves, their academic failure suggests that teachers' teaching approach or lack of establishing caring relationships with the student participants also contributed to these students not achieving.

STUDENT PERCEPTIONS OF OTHER TEACHERS

All the students were asked to describe their relationships with their other teachers, and their responses were very different from those describing their relationships with their favorite teachers. I saw no signs of meaningful relationships other than those with their favorite teachers, and the students appeared to have adjusted to this fact. Matthew selected his words carefully when he described his relationships with other teachers:

> Most of my teachers are good teachers, they...a few of them will go into depth to help you out, but a lot of them basically just read you off the standards and pitch you the lesson and then hope you get it. But there's some

of my teachers who will do all that and then, you know, solve the problem with you over and over again so you know how to do it. Yeah, that, most of them aren't too in depth with you, the student.

One student recounted, "My relationships with my teachers are okay. I sit in class, do my work and speak only when spoken to. I'm not a troublemaker, so yeah, I think my relationships are good." The other seven students responded similarly, indicating that their relationships ranged from "normal, nothing special." to "your typical teacher-student relationship." This should not continue to be their normal experience.

Six of the nine students, who were athletes, credited going to college as their motivation for doing well in their other classes. The other three, who were non-athletes, identified graduation from high school as their motivation. Samuel mentioned that science is the hardest subject for him, and, although he had never failed a class, science is always challenging. When asked to describe his relationship with his science teacher, he stated,

We don't, I don't really talk to her. We don't really have a bond or nothing like that; it's just okay. Do the assignment, turn it in, see you tomorrow. Take notes, take the quiz, take the tests. That's it. Everything's just straightforward, move on.

Fortunately, all these students found something outside of the classroom, such as graduating from high school or moving onto college, to motivate them to remain in their classes.

Each student was also asked how their teachers would describe them. All the descriptions were positive, including "shy," "quiet, "funny," "class clown," "hardworking," "talkative," and "a good student." All the students said they would agree with the description given by the teacher. None of the students expressed any animosity toward their teachers when describing them. They did not report any negative views held by teachers about them either, yet the caring relationships that were developed between the participants and their many teachers were few. Should teachers give clear explanations of what students can expect from them and their schools?

RACE AND CURRICULUM

This section addresses the third and final theme that emerged from the main research questions. Since all of the participants were African American males, understanding their perception of the significance of race in regard to school belonging was essential. Student perceptions of themselves as teachers of African American males and students' perceptions of race and school performance were the two related sub-themes. In the first sub-theme, the participants described how they would interact with African American male students if they were the teacher. This topic was addressed in the interview protocol to discover what participants would consider important qualities and/or strategies for relating to Black male high school students. The second sub-theme participants discussed was the role of race in regard to their academic performance.

Interview questions revealed the perceptions of participants regarding the absence of race in the curriculum. Seven of the nine students reported that they never had a discussion in class regarding a positive contribution made to society by an African American. One student acknowledged having this experience, while another student reported that this had only happened "once." The responses to how they felt about this fact varied.

Three of the nine students appeared apathetic in their responses. Mark commented, "I don't think I'm affected, cuz it's always been that way all of my school years." Like Mark's answer, Luke declared, with a blank face, "It doesn't." Timothy reported that he "was used to it [the lack of positive discussions about his race]." John, quietly and without much emotion, stated, "I think they should teach more about African Americans." Mark's disposition on this question was like John's, while shaking his head from side to side, he simply stated, "It's always been this way; I don't feel nothing."

Paul did not recall if this had ever happened. However, Matthew had a different perspective, While making eye-to-eye contact with me, he expressed, "It's wrong; like, all I can say is…it's just wrong." Silas, like Matthew, expressed strong emotions, "In my opinion, it says we're not important enough to talk about at school." Their responses were interestingly different; some students had very little to say, appearing to recognize the fact that "this is just the way things are" and thus recognizing the status quo aspect of education, while others voiced their dissatisfaction.

Six of the nine students reported never having an assignment or a lesson that focused on African Americans in particular. Seven of nine students reported never reading a book in school about their race. Their feelings regarding this absence were just as strong as their feelings regarding not having any positive discussions about African Americans. A few elaborated on their answers.

One of the students, who reported reading a section of a book that included African Americans, stated, "It's good and bad cuz it felt like the whole class was looking at me, so like I was glad that we was reading it, but it was bad feeling everybody eyes on me."

Matthew paused and looked up to the ceiling for a few seconds before his statement:

Never have assignments about my race. And I read books about my race, but like my teachers never in all years of school have never assigned me a book about my race. But I have read a couple books on my own about it and read online about it, watched TV programs about it, but it's never in the school curriculum.

When asked how he felt about this fact, he continued:

I mean, we are a very important part of this nation. I'm just going to use one example. If you look back on inventions, Black people invented a lot of important things, like, in the past so just that alone should tell you that we're important, and it's sad that there's not one— there's not even a class like African American studies. It could be; I don't see why that couldn't be an elective—

like, we have cooking class, we have yarn class, all that stuff, but we don't have an African American culture class, something like that. We don't have anything like that. Kind of feels like we're being ignored, like we're not, you know, getting the recognition that we deserve, and I really don't know why.

Five of the nine students reported having one teacher who was African American. Their responses to this question were interesting; three of the students seemed to have never really given this fact any thought. As a matter of fact, one student did say that he had never really thought about it. Four of the six students who had a Black teacher stated that there should be more Black teachers. The fifth student explained, "I think this [only having one Black teacher] is bad because there are a lot of teachers at my school." The sixth student reported, "If I had more Black teachers, again I'd be a little bit more influenced about my culture." One student, however, commented on the influence of his football buddy:

Ms. Brody [pseudonym], who is African American, I've had her for, you know, when you're here varsity football, you get assigned a staff member—a football buddy and that's someone you go to, you know, when you just want to talk, when you're just having trouble with something, like a mentor, and I got assigned to her my junior year. And just in these two years we—I've learned so much from her. She's one of those…she's one of those people who, like, in the Black culture, she's like the grandma you go and talk to, and she gives you all these wise quotes. So that's the role she plays in my life, like, I'll go to her, and she give me a bunch of advice, and pat me on the back, and just make me smile.

Three students had never had a Black teacher. Their responses indicated that they had not given this fact much thought.

STUDENT PERCEPTIONS OF THEMSELVES AS TEACHERS OF AFRICAN AMERICAN MALES

None of the participants thought their teachers could do anything to help them feel connected. They were hopeless. Even with wait time, they could not imagine how their teachers could do anything that would effect change. Their answers were the same regarding the principal. One student thought that the principal could help if he put more of them, i.e., Black male students, in the same classes so they would feel comfortable. Although most of the participants could not list anything the teachers or principal could do to help them feel more connected, when they were asked how they would interact with Black male students if the roles were reversed, that is if the participants were the teachers or the principal, their responses were informative.

Each student was asked to imagine being on stage, addressing the teachers at their schools that teach Black boys. One student was not sure what he would say. Another student said he would say, "Don't pick on us so much," and then added, "I would probably tell them to help us with tutors or something to find us a way to where we could understand everything. We need help to get further in life." The other six did not have statements; instead they had questions.

MATTHEW

Before Matthew asked his question, he reported feeling overlooked and ignored; he wanted teachers to identify what Black students were doing wrong. "I'd just ask them what are we doing wrong not to be recognized more in the school?"

MARK

Mark had several questions; he reported being confused about not learning about his culture. He also stated that most teachers do not think Black boys are smart nor take the time to get to know them. He stated, "I would just ask them why they don't teach good stuff about Black people, why they don't think we can be smart, why they don't take the time to get to know us."

LUKE

Luke reported that he wanted teachers to be fair when teaching Black boys, and his questions were reflective, "I'd ask them, 'How are you teaching them [Black male students], what are you teaching them, are you teaching them the same stuff everybody else is learning?'"

JOHN

John questioned how the current teachers would respond to more Black teachers and students and his questions addressed his concern, "Could we have more Black teachers and students at school?"

TIMOTHY

Timothy said that race topics do not come up with teachers, and his questions were directly related to his concern: "I would ask how the Black students act in their class, and how do they feel teaching them?"

DAVID

David's question may sound harsh to some, but during the interview, his facial expressions and tone suggested he was sincere. "Why do they judge Black people before they even know them?"

Most of the students wanted answers from some of the teachers. If they were the principal, they could not think of any information that they wanted to share in that role with their school's teachers. This question caused the participants to pause the longest before answering and was the most difficult one for them to answer.

All the students were able to address this question from a different angle when they were asked to imagine themselves as the teacher and to list what they would do with or for African American male students in their classes. All their answers were centered on building relationships. Matthew reported that he would interact with his students in a way that would build caring relationships; he even saw his role extend beyond the classroom.

> I would make them feel appreciated. I would give them
> a lot of chances to prove themselves. I'd just have a re-
> ally, really good friendship and relationship with them.
> I'd be that teacher that they could come talk to, but at

the same time, I won't take it easy on them, you know. I'll ask them let me see your grades. Why do have a C or a D in this class? You need to get it up. So, I'll kind of play that father role because I know a lot of them don't probably have a father role in their lives, so I'd probably play that role."

Mark, like Matthew, described his interactions as a teacher in caring terms. He made statements of support coupled with accountability. "I would meet them at the door every day and check on them, talk to them about all their classes—not just mine. I would ask them about other things other than school."

Luke was consistent in his responses throughout the interview in regard to more exposure to his culture. He reported that if he were the teacher, he would give something that he did not receive in school. "I would teach them about African American history."

John too thought it was important to build relationships with his Black male students. Although he was not an athlete, he was close enough to them to identify the benefits. "Ask them how they're doing in school and if they needed help with anything. And if they weren't playing sports, I'd ask them. 'Why not?'"

Paul struggled academically, and he described his interactions with Black students in one sentence. "I would help put work in terms that they would know and try to encourage them."

Timothy described his interactions in very similar terms as the above participants. He too mentioned that he would offer students support along with accountability.

That's a good question.... I'd make sure they're doing what they are supposed to do so they could achieve goals, what's right, what's wrong, what's cool, what's not, and how to stay out of kid drama. Don't call, or judge, people on their skin color. There's more that I had in my head, but I just can't say it. I just can't... I think I would help them learn more than other people so they could achieve more. I would tell them to achieve your goals instead of doing what people says Black people do—being lazy and all that stuff they say about us but I want you to be the opposite.

Silas saw a need to be harder on Black males, but it was coupled with support as well. He, like other participants, stressed being available to the students.

I would help them a little bit more because I want to see African Americans be successful, and I would be more strict just because sometimes they [teachers] need to be, you know. They need to be like that. I would just give them extra help, just answering all their questions, before school, after school help, tutoring, a lot of individual help—just stuff like that—just to make sure they know, to understand what I'm talking about.

Samuel described his role with his students similarly to the other participants, adding that he would involve the parents.

"I would be a little harder on them when they didn't get their work done. I would ask them if it was because they didn't understand it or they just didn't want to do it? If they didn't understand it, I would make them come back and see me after school or something, if they didn't want to do it, I would call home or tell a coach if they played a sport."

David spoke in terms outside of school. He mentioned encouraging his students in a different way. "I would take them out to colleges to see what college life is like and motivate them to get good grades."

Interestingly, when participants were asked to identify what teachers and the principal could do to help them feel a sense of belonging, they replied "Nothing." Yet when they were able to describe the type of teacher and principal they would be, they were able to communicate it clearly. In all their statements, their actions are intentional and supportive. The interactive, personal and caring learning environment they described would be considered culturally relevant according to some researchers.

STUDENTS' PERCEPTIONS OF RACE AND SCHOOL PERFORMANCE

Four of nine students reported that being African American and male influences their school performance. Matthew described his thoughts on the subject by sharing the following insight:

I feel like I'm like, I'm inclined to do better just because I'm Black. So, like, I'll go back to the AP class [referenced previously], like, I kind of knew there wasn't going to be a lot of Black people in class, so I thought, *Okay, I'm Black, I got to study and be a good...*You know, good... What's the word? *Example* from my race. I'm going to try even harder. So, I could use that quote basically as my life story in school for the past three or four years, I gotta try harder because I'm Black.

Mark had similar thoughts, "Yeah, sometimes, it makes me work harder because people don't think we smart." Samuel remarked:

Being African American makes me want to work harder because it's going to make a difference in my life, it's going to make a difference maybe ten years from now because [pause] I'm going to be doing something special or something good.

David had similar feelings as the others, expressing them as follows:

A lot of people don't see us Black people as being smart, so you do good it proves them wrong. That's another thing that motivates me, and it just feels good to get good grades also and feel up there with other ethnicities.

Many of the participants spoke openly about their feelings regarding being "the only one" in their classrooms. When discussing the idea of having more Black males attend Island High, many responded that it would be positive because they would be able to relate to more people and have opportunities to hang out with more people of their race. One even mentioned that if he were the principal, he would put more Blacks in the same class in order to help them feel more comfortable. Mark elaborated on his thoughts by adding the following:

> I have Mexican friends, Asian friends, White friends, and of course, Black friends, so I'm cool with everybody. It would just be nice to have more people who like eat the same stuff you eat and do the same stuff to they hair, you know, just relate. But that don't really happen in class, and sometimes, it's, like, lonely. If there was more of us, we could, like, remind each other about tests and stuff and work together when it was, like, time for groups. But I just kinda mind my own business in class.

Although there were varying degrees of school belonging among the participants, all of them felt they belonged to something. The athletes expressed a sense of belonging to their team and the non-athletes to their peers. The students, with favorite teachers, also expressed a sense of belonging in that classroom. It was apparent, in this study, that the existence of belonging influenced the attitudes and actions of some of the participants. More specifically, the teacher-students relationship tended to influence their academic experience. The athletes experienced a larger social network group than non-athletes that included peers as well as adults. The statements from participants and final grades in classes with a favorite teacher indicated increased academic performance. However, there was no evidence that the participants made a correlation between their relationship with teachers and their academic engagement and performance. All the participants expressed that more cultural representation in the school curriculum along with more African American males would increase their sense of school belonging.

Three of the participants were seniors and six were juniors. During the time of the interview, the participants had between 30 and 40 teachers, considering they have six teachers per semester, some were duplicated for year-long courses. Nevertheless, only six of the nine identified a favorite teacher who had made an impact on them personally and academically. The teachers who were engaging and caring appeared to demonstrate cultural relevancy in a manner that yielded an increase in academic performance in that particular class.

CONCLUSIVE FINDINGS

This study's main finding was that caring teacher-student relationships seemed to result in improved student academic engagement and performance. This finding is consistent with documented research.[3] For example, when students interpreted a teacher's actions to be caring, that nurturing attitude influenced their academic engagement and achievement in that classroom. In some cases, the influence of this relationship altered the student's overall attitude toward academics and school.

I found this attitude exemplified by Matthew who stated, "Now, I actually like school; I like learning. I like being in the classroom and interacting with the teacher and having intelligent conversations with the teacher. So yeah, she [his favorite teacher] changed me." Some participants articulated their excitement about learning and gave examples of their learning; some were even motivated to sustain and strengthen their newfound senses of self-efficacy about learning.

Silas, a senior, had his favorite teacher his sophomore year and was so proud of his academic accomplishments that he stated, "I probably get a transcript like two or three times a month just to see what my grades are even though they really don't changed; I just like looking at my transcripts."

Conversely, the participants' relationships with other teachers were not as positive and did not yield the same positive academic results, such as engaging learning experiences and above average grades. Many of the participants were disconnected from their other teachers and the subject matter they taught. This fact was not only evident when participants described their interactions with other teachers, but also evident in the lack of classroom participation they self-reported. The interviews also revealed that many of the students did not expect positive teacher-student relationships and perceived the rarity of these kinds of relationships as being normal. Another finding also included the difference in school belonging that the athlete participants felt, depending on whether their sport was in season. There were obvious differences in school experiences, such as in academic support for athletes versus non-athletes. Furthermore, this study revealed that the African American male athlete participants had a better chance of continuing education at a college or university than the African American male students who were not athletes. Additionally, this study found that the participants had similar feelings regarding the lack of representations of their culture and race in their curriculum.

STUDENTS' PERCEPTIONS OF THEIR SCHOOL

Overall, the participants shared positive perceptions of Island High. Their remarks ranged from optimistic descriptions of peers to general remarks about the competitive history of the sports program. All participants stated that socializing was their favorite interest at school. All mentioned positive experiences with their peers and looked forward to meeting with their same group every day. For some, their perception of their school belonging was strongly connected to their satisfaction with their peer group. When the participants were asked questions that referenced their school, most of them responded that they defined school more as social setting; a few referenced the size of the school. Once descriptions were given of their school, questions regarding school belonging were introduced.

For most of the participants, school belonging was a different matter. Some felt a sense of belonging because of the students they knew; some experienced a sense of belonging because of the sport they played. Others did not feel they belonged at all.

The participants who were athletes showed signs of belonging to their team. However, one athlete, Matthew, pointed out that he did not feel a sense of belonging at all after football season. This student as well as the other eight participants was not active in any other school activities or groups. The athlete participants hung out together every day during break and lunch, and according to the participants, this was their safe space. It was familiar, and it was understood by the students and faculty that this space belonged to them.

STUDENTS' PERCEPTIONS OF THEIR RELATIONSHIPS AND INTERACTIONS WITH THEIR TEACHERS

According to the research, the environments that are created by successful teachers of African American students are relational and personal.[4] The relational and personal environments that were created for the participants, by their favorite teachers, created a foundation for academic engagement. Creating environments that include high expectations of caring relationships with, and respectful treatment of students are identifiable strategies, which are employed by successful teachers of African American students.[5] The six participants who acknowledged having a favorite teacher commented on the caring interactions they had with that particular teacher. The participants in the study attributed their improved classroom participation to the motivation to learn that was ignited by their favorite teacher.

CARING AS A COMPONENT OF BELONGING

The participants' motivation to learn and engage appeared to be by-products of the positive relationships initiated by these teachers. This type of relationship has been established as caring. All the students, who reported having a favorite teacher, interpreted the actions of the teacher as *caring*.[6] According to the participants, encouragement from their favorite teachers not only inspired them with a desire to academically engage but also helped them to build a sense of academic confidence. As Matthew declared,

> Like in English class, I'll probably come off as a shy, quiet kid, but now when it's time for me to stand up and talk to the class or present something or read out loud, I'll confront it with power, and that' how I am now.

In each case, the student participants' academic performance improved as a result. The caring relationship that was facilitated by these teachers appeared to influence the learning experiences of the student participants in a way that inspired them to engage and excel. Learning, motivation, and encouragement are maximized when the need to belong is met.[7] The participants, who expressed a sense of belonging in their favorite teachers' classroom, seemed to understand that sense of belonging stemmed from their teacher's care for them.

Matthew, Mark and John stated that their favorite teacher consistently expressed confidence in their academic abilities. The students in the current study were active participants in the classrooms of their favorite teachers; they spoke of having confidence when they raised their hands, asking and answering questions, and contributing to class discussions. The focus of this study was academic performance rather than achievement; nevertheless, the data showed that when participants failed or struggled academically in a particular class, an element of care was missing from their relationship with that particular teacher and as reported by the participants there was a decline in class participation and performance. Students in the study performed better in the classrooms where they perceived the teacher as taking a personal interest in them as students.

Six of the participants experienced a sense of belonging with their favorite teachers' classroom. For instance, Matthew reported that his favorite teacher shared a life-changing experience with the class when she explained her open-heart surgery and all the complications that followed. He stated that she told the class that her story is only one example of perseverance and assured them of the success to which they could look forward if they embraced challenges and worked hard. This sharing of personal information set the tone for the class, and several students reported feeling connected to the teacher as a result because, as Mark stated, "Teachers don't hardly tell you things about themselves."

The participants in this study also expressed pride in earning above average grades on assignments, quizzes, and tests; however, these same students described their experiences in other classes differently. Some reported only answering questions when they were called upon; others stated that they would answer only if they were sure they had the right answer. For these participants, the lack of engagement negatively influenced their academic performance. Within these same classrooms, the perceived lack of caring student-teacher relationships as described by the students, appeared to affect the students' attitudes regarding engagement as well as their academic confidence in the classroom.

According to Timothy and other student participants, the learning environments in the other teachers' classrooms were not conducive to their participating freely. When Timothy was asked why he did not participate in other classrooms, he responded, "Honestly, too shy or embarrassed to raise my hand to ask for help or I feel that I might get judged or something."

From the participants' perspective, participation appeared to involve taking a risk when school belonging was lacking. In this current study, student participation, which is often referred to as engagement, was sparked by a teacher's warmth and caring.

Environments with caring teachers help children to flourish. The participants in this study, who had a favorite teacher, experienced a combination of belonging in their favorite teacher's classroom and a sense of caring on their teacher's behalf. These phenomena influenced the students' regarding the subject matter and their academic ability. Two of the students earned their first "A" in high school history in the class with their favorite teacher. They credited the encouragement they received from each of their favorite teachers as the impetus for their academic performance.

A positive correlation exists between belonging and academic performance. Where a caring teacher-student relationship existed, academic engagement followed. As a result, these students were able to experience academic success in courses that they previously considered their least favorite.

BELONGING EVIDENCED IN LEARNING

One of the more surprising findings in this study was that three of the participants stated that their favorite teacher taught their least favorite subject, yet they all received grades of B or better, and their attitudes regarding the subject matter also changed. Their favorite teachers' approach to learning was mentioned by several students during the interview.

Silas asserted, "Her way of approaching the lesson was a lot better than I had had before." Samuel stated, "We worked in groups; she taught us how to help each other." While these participants were pleased with their end of year course grades, they spoke more about how it felt to learn in this particular class. Mark exclaimed,

> I paid attention in her class cuz she thought I was smart, and it felt good to get asked questions and know the answers. And I knew what to study for to make good grades on tests. Yeah, she made me feel smart in class.

The above student comment is consistent with Guy L. Cornell and L. Rev. Wellborn's research suggesting that when students perceive that their teachers view them as academically capable, they respond by demonstrating advanced levels of achievement.[8] For instance, Matthew expressed that English was his "worse" subject because he struggled with writing, but after the nurturing experience with his favorite teacher, who taught his least favorite subject in tenth grade, he was placed in AP English (in twelfth grade), enjoyed the challenge of writing essays, and was earning an A- at the time of the interview. The students' success in what was previously his most challenging subject was the by-product of a caring teacher-student relationship coupled with what seemed to be effective teaching strategies. Matthew not only earned above average grades but also scored advanced on the state test in English Language Arts the previous year.

This study suggests that strategies to close the achievement gap for Black males should include relationship building and culturally relevant teaching. Although the favorite teachers were successful in developing positive relationships with their students through caring, caring alone is not enough to yield the academic success that is needed. Teachers must merge academic rigor, high expectations, and effective teaching strategies, with caring teacher relationships to facilitate learning as a way to begin to close the achievement gap for African American males.

Those teachers who took the time and made the student himself as well as his learning a priority impacted the participant's academic lives. When students perceive their teachers as supportive and encouraging, the students' academic engagement and performance increases, and this study shows that when a caring relationship is formed between teacher and student, the student often responds by becoming academically engaged. The participants' engagement was a response to teacher interaction. In other words, student learning is highly dependent upon the relationship that is established between student and teacher. Therefore, it is critical that teachers are aware of the important role they play in the academic outcomes for Black males by establishing caring relationships with them. According to the interview data, the participants' relationships with the favorite teachers were frequent and consistent and intentionally maintained by the teachers.

Research reveals that exemplary Black teachers teach in a manner that improves the academic and personal well-being of Black students.[9] Interestingly, in this study, three of four participants' favorite teachers were Black. Each participant, who stated that he had a favorite teacher, gave examples of how the teachers expressed their academic and personal concern for them. In addition, each of the participants reported, and their transcripts confirmed that they had improved academically while they were enrolled in their favorite teacher's course.

Data gathered by Gloria Ladson-Billings argues that because culturally relevant teachers are serious advocates for their students, the walls of their classrooms do not limit their advocacy.[10] There is no evidence that the favorite teachers identified by participants in the current study were purposely implementing culturally relevant teaching methods; however, their interactions with the student participants showed patterns similar to the types of culturally inclusive interactions found within the literature, such as those noted by Ladson-Billing.

An example of a teacher's advocacy that extended beyond her classroom would be when one of Matthew's favorite teachers stopped reading one of his essays in class to move him to AP English. Matthew explained that while the teacher was individually meeting with students to give them feedback on their essays, he patiently waited for his turn. The teacher asked him if anyone had assisted him with his paper, and after he replied "no," she picked up the phone to call the AP English teacher in the middle of their conversation. Matthew was immediately placed in the AP class, and the teacher personally completed the paperwork with the counselor later that day. This teacher recognized Matthews' potential and was proactive about placing him in the most rigorous classroom.

BELONGING AS A PRODUCT OF STUDENT-TEACHER CONNECTION

The participants also reported several instances where each of their favorite teachers showed an interest in them outside of the normal classroom hours or domain. For example, one of the teachers supported the athletes by attending their sporting events. Another teacher limited the amount of homework she gave them in order to gain buy-in from the students and get them to focus in class. Other favorite teachers inquired about the participants' academic status in other classes and, sometimes, made appointments with the students to give them extra help before or after school.

Another teacher shared what it was like to grow up in the projects with Paul, one of the participants, and he reported, "It let me know that if he can make it out of the projects, I can too." This conversation was a turning point for Paul; he began to engage in this teacher's class and earned his first A. The message that this student received from his favorite teacher was that he was not only concerned about Paul's doing well in his classes but was also concerned about Paul's overall academic success and personal well-being.

Decision-making and developing a code of ethics or guiding principles is acritical life skill but may not necessarily be a part of school curriculum. Nevertheless, the participants' favorite teachers understood the value of these skills as they related to the overall development of these students. Silas, for instance, mentioned that his favorite teacher taught him "right from wrong."

Some of the participants shared examples of how their teachers contributed to their increased self-confidence and self-worth. An increase in a student's self-confidence and an enhanced sense of self-worth are by-products of belonging. For example, Mark stated that he believed his teacher really cared about him because of the interest she displayed in his sport, and he reported feeling a "connection" with her early in the school year.

Paul experienced an increase in self-confidence after Mr. Brown, who was also African American, shared past experiences that were very similar to Paul's. As a result, he stated, "Mr. Brown made me believe my life could change, and I'm different in his class." The combination of this teacher's race, gender and cultural relevancy inspired motivation in a student who had never previously earned a grade higher than a "C" in his high school history.

Cultural competency should accompany the teachers who are identified as highly qualified. Some of the students reported that their other teachers were competent, but it was not reflected in their learning experience. If a teacher is competent in their subject matter but is unaware of how race affects teaching and learning, the Black male (as well as other minorities) probably will continue to be left behind academically. The participants who reported having a favorite teacher also described a strong sense of belonging in their favorite teacher's class as a result of their relationship.

Mentioning that the current study revealed that most of the favorite teachers (three out of the four) shared the same race as the students and that the students seemed to excel academically within these teachers' classrooms is important. This finding appears to suggest that student-teacher identification in terms of race may be a factor in the instruction of Black male high school students. However, sharing the same race does not guarantee a cultural match.

Authentically connecting with students, regardless of race and ethnicity must be intentional. "Even African American teachers need as much professional development as non-Black teachers in ensuring the academic and cultural successes of the African American child."[11]

We see this connecting demonstrated as the students also identified with another teacher, Mrs. McKarrel, who seemed to take a caring, personal interest with the students as people and making sure to provide access to their curriculum. She was not racially the same as the students but seemed to exhibit some of the characteristics that Ladson-Billings identify as culturally relevant. The caring relationship also served as access to the curriculum.

SAME STUDENTS, DIFFERENT TEACHERS, DIFFERENT ENGAGEMENT AND PERFORMANCE

The importance of caring teacher-student relationships is not a new concept. A work of essays published by the founder of the school of individual psychology, Alfred Adler revealed the author believed that students unconnected to the school community, to others in the school, and particularly to the teacher could usually explain school failure. Since the primary members of a school community are teachers and students, the need for belonging cannot be met without the student's experiencing a level of attachment to the teacher. The data also suggests that the most important element in feeling a sense of school belonging is the individual classroom experience that is influenced by the relationship created between teacher and student. This teacher-student relationship highly influences the teaching and learning that occurs. In other words, this relationship determines the level of student's expectation and support, as well as their engagement and performance.[12]

Consistent with Osterman's findings, six of the nine students in the present study failed at least one class his freshman year, and all of them reported not having a relationship with the teacher in the particular class that they failed. Researcher Urie Bronfenbrenner identifies the dynamics between teacher and student as the primary instrument for learning and human development.[13] The interaction between teacher and student determined or highly influenced student learning. The student's relationship with the teacher determined if the climate was positive or negative. This study validated the premise that the optimal learning environment is not created when there is little or no communication between the teacher and student. There was a noticeable difference in the students' engagement in each of their favorite teacher's class versus their engagement in other teachers' classrooms; the difference seemed to be in the quality of teachers' relationship with their student. These differences not only were manifested in student engagement, but also were evident in student learning and academic performance, which were evidenced in students' final grades. Clearly, other factors may be involved when students are not academically successful.

A significant relationship also exists between achievement and engagement. In the absence of caring teachers, many of the participants earned average (C) and below average (D) grades and reported sitting in the classroom bored, watching the clock, and waiting for bell to ring. These same participants reported having insignificant relationships with teachers, other than their favorite teachers, that did not include conversations. One student reported, for example, that he was failing science and had never had a conversation with his science teacher. He defined this relationship as a "typical teacher-student relationship." When asked to describe this typical relationship, he added,

> We don't... I don't really talk to her. We don't have a bond or nothing like that, it's just...okay, do the assignment, turn it in, see you tomorrow, take notes, take the quiz, take the test, that's it. Everything is straightforward, move on.

Similarly, another participant failed math and reported that he had never spoken in class or with the teacher about anything. When Samuel was asked to describe his relationship with this particular teacher, he replied, "It's your normal teacher relationship, nothing special." The interview data reflected several similar comments made by the other participants in similar situations. These students appeared to have systematically experienced classroom practices and school cultures that have led them to conclude and accept that lack of caring relationships with teachers is the norm. Although this reality negatively impacts them as students, they have come to perceive it as the way it is.

Research published by Dena Swanson, Michael Cunningham, and Margaret Spencer states that youth often expect teachers and other staff to be supportive of their development[14]; however, the participants in this study gave no indication of this sort of expectation. As a matter of fact, they appeared surprised when teachers took an interest in them and their learning and cared about them as individuals. One student expressed, "I don't know how she does it, but she actually takes time to teach everyone and answer questions so that everybody gets to learn." This statement of surprise may be a result of a phenomenon that Swanson suggests exists, i.e., when African American males do not receive positive academic reinforcement that supports their individual goals and development, they may actively decide not to expect it from schools. In other words, perhaps when the expected support from their teachers did not materialize, this expectation of the participants gradually declined as a result of unmet expectations. Another student characterized his teacher as "nice" and considered her a smart teacher, but he still failed the class. Unfortunately, the teaching methods employed by teachers carry little significance when the need for belonging is not satisfied at first.

The failure on the part of the teacher to address the participants' need for belonging was evident in the classes that some of the participants failed in ninth grade and other grades. None of the participants accused their teachers of not knowing their subject matter, but they did report that they did not have relationships with the teachers of those classes. Surely, other factors besides the lack of a caring relationship may have contributed to failure, but research evidences a stronger teacher relationship may have helped them overcome other obstacles.

This need to belong at school is met primarily by a positive relationship with the teacher. The participants in the study did not appear to understand the correlation between their relationships with their teachers and their classroom experience; however, there was a decline in student learning, engagement, and performance when a relationship with their teacher did not generate a sense of belonging within the student.

Children who felt nurtured at school believed in the value of their work, had higher expectations of their own success, and were motivated when they felt they belonged.[15] The participants' need for belonging seem to be unmet in most classrooms due to a lack of positive relationships with their teachers. The participants did not report this as a negative experience;

rather, they discussed it as if it were to be expected. Even when participants failed a class, they blamed themselves and not the teacher, as if the complete burden of student learning rested on their shoulders.

THE ATHLETE AND NON-ATHLETE DIVIDE

The social and academic benefits to being an athlete were obvious. Students who are involved in school activities have higher levels of school connection and membership. This fact was evident in the current study in that the athletes experienced a larger social network that included peers and additional staff members, such as AVID teachers, coaches, and mentors. The participants who were in AVID were also athletes. Additional programs, such as AVID, provided opportunities for athletes, in this study to have formal and informal interactions with adult staff members. For example, the AVID program provided college field trips, which enabled the participants to socialize with adults in a less formal setting. In addition, personal tours and college contacts exposed the students to the potential reality of going to college. Participants experienced the social benefits of being popular with their peers as well as having access to adults on campus for additional relational and academic support.

The popularity and status of being an athlete even earned them the privilege of a designated "space" on campus. Not only do they consider the space as their own, but others also refer to the space as the "football bench." All the participants identified a place where they socialized during break and lunch.

However, the non-athletes mentioned two or three friends in their space, whereas the athletes mentioned the football bench, which was a popular location with a large group of more athletes and other visitors. Not only did the athletes socialize there, it was also popular for other students to be associated with this area because of the status attached to the football bench.

None of the athletes had a discipline file, while two of the three non-athletes had several incidents that resulted in referrals. This is another example of the different school experiences between the student athletes and non-athletes. Interestingly, the same two participants with the lowest state test scores were also the non-athletes who had the lowest grade point averages. Moreover, their only connections to school were their friends.

Three of the nine students in the study had an adult on campus with whom they would talk if they had a problem. None of the adults were teachers. One of the adults on campus was a counselor (identified by an athlete), the other was a security guard (identified by a non-athlete), and the last was a football buddy, an adult who volunteered to be teamed with a football player for mentoring purposes.

The athletes in the study referred to the counselor as the sports counselor, although this was not her official title. Nevertheless, she was known for assisting the athletes with school related issues. Both athletes, Matthew and David, identified an adult on campus with whom they developed relationships through sports; the non-athlete mentioned the security guard, a relationship that began with discipline issues but developed over time.

EXTRA SUPPORTS FOR ATHLETES

In addition to the privilege of having a designated space of their own, the athletes were assigned staff mentors who served as additional support. Matthew mentioned that knowing that his mentor, a football buddy, was on campus was helpful. Although the football buddy was not a teacher, she was African American, and the athlete credited her with giving him wise advice and giving him pats on the back. Matthew perceived her as the "grandma type." She was someone he trusted, and she always made him "feel better" after they talked.

The academic benefits to being an athlete included the AVID class that equipped students with college information along with personalized college preparation. This class also offered specific guidance in the area of a-g courses, placement in these courses as well as advanced placement courses, study skills training, homework assistance by peers and college students who served as tutors, assistance with college applications and parent education nights, which included financial aid information. According to the athletes, they were enrolled in the program by a coach and counselor once they made a team. The additional information, guidance, and encouragement, given to athletes, through AVID provided academic and other advantages that the non-athletes in this study did not have.

The advantages of this additional information between the two groups became apparent when it came to their aspirations. All the athletes expressed intentions to go to a university after high school. In contrast, only one of the three non-athletes mentioned wanting to go to Temple Community College, while the other two just wanted to get out of high school. The athletes had academic goals and aspirations that developed over time, and the sports program assisted them in developing these ambitions. Some of the participants mentioned that at some point, the sport-mandated grade checks were their only motivation to perform well academically. This study is not suggesting that participation in athletics is the answer to addressing this significant achievement gap experienced by African American high school males; however, participation in athletics, along with built-in academic supports, appeared to provide the athlete participants with the personal guidance they needed to navigate high school and prepare for college or university attendance.

RACE AND CURRICULUM

LACK OF CULTURAL REPRESENTATION WITHIN CURRICULUM

When asked about the representation of culture in the curriculum, all the participants voiced a desire to learn about their culture in school. Seven of the nine participants stated that they neither had a conversation about a positive contribution made by someone of their same race nor had an assignment regarding their race. When asked if they had ever read a book about their race, Matthew responded, "[I] never have assignments about my race. Like, my teachers in all my years of school have never assigned me a book about my race, I've read some on my own, but it's never in the school curriculum." In response to the same question, Silas added the following:

> I think that like if we had a class or Black people were in books for good stuff, it would make us take more pride in our culture, and yeah, we could be in class smiling for a change when people talk about Black people.

Similarly, Mark stated, "I think if we had a class about our culture, I honestly think, like, that would make us appreciate our race more and do better." John was a little more neutral or unaffected. "It's been like this forever; I'm use to it."

When asked how to describe how they would feel about more Black males attending Island High, all the participants expressed a desire for more presence of Black males and teachers so that they would feel more comfortable at school. Two of the participants stated that Black teachers "understood" them in a way that other teachers did not and that having more Black males would provide more opportunities to share cultural commonalities. The participants also mentioned the social isolation that they experienced due to a lack of other Black students in the class.

David stated that in many of his classes, he is the only Black student, and even after three years in the same school, sometimes he still feels "lonely." Samuel claimed that having more Black males would help them feel "more like a unit." Their comments suggest that a genuine struggle is taking place at this institution to embrace, develop and celebrate African

American cultural identities and that only a few teachers have been able to assist them in this area. Of course, site administration oftentimes cannot control the racial diversity of staff and student enrollment, but culturally relevant curriculum can be implemented if effective professional development is provided.

The observation that the participants, as Black students, expressed a desire to take African American courses and to see more of their own cultural history in their classes is important to note. Researchers state that people of color would be less invisible in academia if schools' curriculum were infused with contributions of people of color and that this infusion would assist African American males in finding their place in education by countering negative stereotypes.[16]

Ladson-Billings argues that when the dominant culture continues to adopt textbooks or curriculum that distorts or omits another culture's history, the only way to counter the negative affects is for schools to embed that culture within the curriculum. Culturally relevant curriculum can validate other students' culture. The students in the present study expressed feeling invisible as a result of the lack of presence of their culture and race in the curriculum.

In order to ensure that all children receive a quality education, the experiences of all races should be included in the schools' curriculum. Timothy described a disadvantage to the lack of his culture in the curriculum by stating, "We need to see good things our people did and made, but yeah, White people need to know too. If it ain't in schoolbooks, how they gone know?" It is important for African American students, particularly males, to have a deep awareness of past and current struggles for educational access and opportunities; this kind of awareness has historically promoted a strong value for learning and education in the African American community.[17]

Within the context of this study, the participants were at a disadvantage, since it appears that the African American community in the catchment area of Island School District is small and scattered. Nevertheless, schools can address the need of African American males by incorporating culturally relevant curriculum in the school with carefully planned professional development programs that focus on teacher action research and offers appropriate teacher support. The professional development program should explain why and demonstrate how to implement a culturally relevant curriculum as well as reap its benefits for the students.

IMPLICATIONS FOR POLICY AND PRACTICE

The findings of this research study indicate a need for a series of professional development experiences with teachers in the area of relationship building. The professional development plan would need to include strategies for implementation, with effective teacher coaching to improve teacher-student relationships with African American male students. Opposition and resistance to the above noted idea of teacher caring and culturally relevant teaching should be expected, and resources should be put in place to assist teachers. This professional development program can positively contribute to the overall educational experience of African American males by increasing their sense of school belonging, academic engagement, academic performance, academic achievement, and personal development.

Another implication involves professional development in cultural relevancy, which may include developing the characteristics of culturally relevant teachers, as well as understanding the benefit of cultural relevant teaching and culturally relevant curriculum. Educators should have healthy conversations about effective strategies that build academic confidence in African American males and about the impact of a curriculum that displays positive contributions from other African Americans along with their rich heritage of struggle for education has on African American male students.[18]

Indeed, the race of students and the cultural background of teachers play a significant role in the education of Black students. Therefore, recognizing that race and the cultural relevancy of the teacher, influences teaching and learning is critical to the academic success of African American male students. Teachers should be given the information and resources to address this critical fact through professional development. It is important to frame the professional development as a reform of the system instead of another inadequate program that seeks to reform the students. This information should bring awareness to the powerful influence of teacher-student relationships as well as the connection between this relationship and academic engagement and performance.[19]

The findings of this study suggest that there is a need for

schools to provide additional academic supports for non-athletes. One solution could be to consider student interest and create student-centered clubs and organizations led by caring adults. The non-athletes did not report having positive relationships with other adults on campus, except for their relationships with their favorite teachers. Also, they were less knowledgeable about the requirements for university attendance, were tracked into lower level courses, were not enrolled in any other school programs or clubs and expressed fewer ambitions and future aspirations. Conversely, the athletes in this study seemed to benefit from what researchers call a *triangulation of influences*, [20] that is those who contributed to the development and building of the athletes' self-efficacy skills, those who held high expectations of the students, and those who were the students' advocates.

CHAPTER FIVE

CONCLUSION

This qualitative research study intended to gain a deeper understanding of the perceptions of school belonging from the perspective of African American high school males. Findings from this study suggest that the student participants who were athletes experienced social and academic benefits that non-athlete student participants did not experience. That students who are involved in school activities have higher levels of school connection and membership was evident in this current study. Another finding of the study suggests that when a caring teacher can facilitate student learning and initiates a relationship with an African American male student, the student reciprocates with becoming more academically engaged and his academic performance improves.

Focusing on the influential nature of the teacher-student relationship, the interactions between teachers and students, and the powerful implications of these interactions on student achievement can serve as a valuable source of professional development knowledge for educators. It is imperative that teachers, who are entrusted with the goal of educating all students are informed and coached to understand the influential nature of caring, teacher-student relationships. Moreover, the relevance of race and learning needs to be critical to teaching African American students in today's schools. If not, Black male students will continue to be forced to find a way to "beat the odds" in order to experience academic success.

Within the current study, commonalities surfaced among all the participants. For example, all the participants had a goal of graduating from high school and had a personal knowledge of the potential consequences of not furthering their education. Some of the consequences included limitations on the quality of life, the possibility of unemployment and low-paying jobs and a diminished sense of self-worth. Some of these students drew these types of consequences from personal examples and lessons passed down from people they knew, while others seemed to be more aware of the broader social context of the experiences of many Black males within their community and society in general. Several students stated that the above consequences coupled with caring relationships with peers and adults were motivating enough for them to attend and complete high school and avoid becoming another dropout statistic. While the consequences noted could be attributed to any group of students who do not take their academic pursuits seriously, the students included in this study internalized these consequences as ones that were more characteristic outcomes for Black students, especially males.

The outcomes of the interviews with these students seem to highlight several considerations for furthering teachers' practices related to African American students. The first of the considerations that emerged through the interviews in this study was that all the students in the study seemed to do better when they perceived themselves as being engaged by their teachers. In each case, it was not simply that the students were completing work within the classrooms; rather, it appeared that their teachers purposely encouraged and sometimes even prodded the students into becoming involved in their own education. Students who were doing the best academically in the study were also those students who reported having close, caring relationships with their teachers and being engaged by them.

This finding has interesting research possibilities in examining patterns of interaction between students and those teachers the students considered to be caring and engaging who were included in the study. This finding may yield more information about what types of teacher interaction patterns are most likely to be interpreted by Black students as engaging. However, the recurrent theme that stood out as reported by the participants was the interpersonal relationship building skills of the teachers who seemed to specifically reach out to the Black males in the study.

The next consideration was arguably the most important finding of the interviews conducted as part of this study. This consideration revealed the need to prepare teachers to be more than state certified; the results seem to indicate that teachers who are culturally proficient seem to create relationships and learning environments that foster a sense of belonging where Black males academically respond and excel. While most of the teachers in this study were also Black, Mrs. McKarrel was not. She was described as relating to the students in a similar manner and taking a similar interest in the students, as did the teachers who were Black. The awareness that this non-Black teacher had regarding the recognition of students' needs was consistent with actions demonstrating cultural relevancy. Whether the teacher was specifically trained in cultural relevancy was not known; however, the culturally relevant actions of this teacher indicate that teachers do not have to share the same racial background as their students in order to be effective in their caring.

The participants in this study responded to a particular type of teacher and teaching style, not because the students had deficits that could not be addressed by other teachers, but the student participants perceived that the favorite teachers cared about them. This perception of care served as motivation and encouragement to engage in the classroom and the overall process of learning. The interview data from this study seems to suggest that teaching students regardless of race, by using a mainstream curriculum, is a strategy that fails to capitalize on the opportunity to create an environment where race is specifically included in the classroom and considered as an important part of understanding students for instructional purposes.

The students within the study expressed that they felt like the quality of their education depended on the teacher to whom they were assigned. While they seemed to take responsibility for their part in the educational process, admitting sometimes to "mess" around in class or not complete all assignments, the student participants also expressed that they were willing to do more for those teachers who seemed to reach out to them. This connection included more than reaching out academically, as the teacher behaviors described by the students seemed to be characteristic of caring about the students as individuals, as well as students. In the absence of a caring relationship, the curriculum in the classroom seemed to be inaccessible to the students across their school experience.

When students within the current study felt engaged, culturally recognized and cared for, they ultimately expressed that they felt they belonged in the academic environment where access to learning was initiated by caring and supportive teachers. This sort of teacher-driven intentional caring that leads to belonging is what educators should seek to achieve when educating African American males.

CHAPTER SIX

MOVING FROM ACKNOWLEDGMENT TO ADVOCACY

DISTRICT LEADERSHIP

In an effort to improve academic achievement for Black boys, District Leadership can:

- Use state and district assessments to disaggregate achievement data by subgroups.

- Complete a comparison analysis of Black males' achievement with other subgroups.

- Write the narrative of the data. Paint a clear picture of current and past performance.

- Set SMART (Specific, measurable, achievable, relevant, time-based) goals related to needed change

- Identify funding needed and allocate it.

- Create and implement a strategic attainment plan ie professional development and implementation plan

- Create an avenue for Black male voices regarding their educational experience to be considered as valuable data.

SITE LEADERSHIP

- Use state and district assessments to disaggregate achievement data by subgroups.
- Complete a comparison analysis of Black males' achievement with other subgroups.
- Write the narrative of the data. Paint a clear picture of current and past performance.
- Set SMART (Specific, measurable, achievable, relevant, time-based) goals related to needed change
- Identify funding needed and allocate it.
- Create and implement a strategic attainment plan, i.e., professional development and implementation plan
- Create an avenue for Black male voices regarding their educational experience to be considered as valuable data.
- Consider instituting cultural proficiency training.

TEACHER

- Recognize personal biases.
- Develop positive relationships with Black males.
- Develop a cultural awareness regarding Black males and their educational experiences.
- Generate and review relevant data connected to Black male perceptions about their learning experiences.
- Create a learning environment that promotes healthy dialogue, trust and respect.
- Consider instituting cultural proficiency training.

END NOTES

INTRODUCTION
[1]Gilberto Q. Conchas, *The Color of Success: Race and High-Achieving Urban Youth* (New York: Teachers College Press, 2003).

CHAPTER ONE
WHY BELONGING MATTERS
[1]Andy Hargreaves, Lorna Earl, and Jim Ryan. *Schooling for Change: Reinventing Education for Early Adolescents.* Bristol, Penna.: Falmer Press, 1996.

[2]Gail C. Furman, "Postmodernism and Community in Schools: Unraveling the Paradox" *Sage Journals,* August 1, 1998, https://journals.sagepub.com/doi/10.1177/0013161X98034003003.

[3]Michelle Fine, "Framing Dropouts: Notes on the Politics of an Urban Public High School," Suny Series, Teacher Empowerment and School Reform (Albany: Suny Press,1991); Donna Y. Ford and J. John Harris, *Multicultural Gifted Education* (New York: Teachers College Press, 1999); Sonia Nieto, Affirming Diversity: The Sociopolitical Context of Multicultural Education (London: Longman, 1992); Michele

Sola and Adrian T. Bennett, "The Struggle for Voice: Narrative, Literacy and Consciousness in an East Harlem School," Sage Journals, January 1, 1985, https://journals.sagepub.com/doi/10.1177/002205748516700107.

[4]Andrea T. J. Ross, Angela M. Powell, and Richard C. Henriksen, Jr., "Self-Identity: A Key to Black Student Success," 2016, *Vistas Online,* https://www.counseling.org/docs/default-source/vistas/article_64ce5528f16116603abcacff0000bee5e7.pdf?sfvrsn=6, accessed October 1, 2019.

[5]National Center for Education Statistics, "Education Achievement and Black-White Inequality (NCES 2001-061)" Office of Educational Research and Improvement (Washington, D.C.: U.S. Department of Education, 2003); Education Trust, "African-American Achievement in America" Retrieved August 8, 2010, from http://www2.edtrust,org/NR/rdonlyres/9AB4AC88-7301-43FF-81A3-EB94807B917F/0/Af Amer_Achievement.pdf.

[6]Thomas Bailey, David Jenkins, and Timothy Leinback, "Community College Low-income and Minority Student Completion Study: Descriptive Statistics from the 1992 High School Cohort." Columbia University College Research Center (New York: Teachers College Press, 2005); Bryan J. Cook and Diana I. Cordova, "Minorities in Higher Education. Twenty-second Annual Status Report" (Washington, D.C.: American Council on Education, 2006).

[7]U. S. Department of Education, "The Condition of Education 2006 (NCES 2006-071)," National Center for Education Statistics, Washington, D.C.: U. S. Government Printing Office, 2006.

[8]California Standardized Testing and Reporting (STAR)

Program, September 22, 2006, https://star.cde.ca.gov/star2006/ Viewreport.asp.

[9]Conchas, *The Color of Success*; Michael Holzman, "Public Education and Black Male Students: The 2006 State Report Card" Schott Educational Inequity Index (Cambridge: The Schott Foundation for Public Education, 2006).

[10]M. Holzman, "Public Education and Black Male Students: The 2006 State Report Card. Schott Educational Inequity Index," Cambridge, Mass.: The Schott Foundation for Public Education, 2006.

[11]U.S. Department of Education, National Center for Education Statistics. "The Condition of Education 2006" (NCES 2006-071). Washington, DC: U.S. Government Printing Office, 2006.

[12]*Ibid.*

[13]Ralph Gardner and Carolyn Talbert-Johnson, "School Reform and Desegregation: The Real Deal or More of the Same?" *Semantic Scholar*, DOI:10.1177/0013124500331007, 2000; Valerie E. Lee, Linda F. Winfield, and Thomas C. Wilson, "Academic Behaviors Among High-Achieving African-American Students, *Sage Publications*, https://doi.org/10.1177/0013124591024001006 1991; U.S. Department of Education, Office for Civil Rights, Annual Report to Congress: Fiscal Years 2001 and 2002, Washington, D.C., 2003.

[14]Bateman, M., & Kennedy, E. (1997). Male African Americans, Single Parent Homes, and Educational Plans: Implications for Educators and Policymakers. Journal of Education for Students Placed at Risk (JESPAR), 2(3), 229-250.

[15]Chinwe J. Uwah, H. George McMahon, Ph.D., and Carolyn F.

Furlow, Ph.D., "School Belonging, Educational Aspirations, and Academic Self-Efficacy Among African American Male High School Students: Implications for School Counselors, *Sage Journals*, Retrieved from https://doi.org/10.1177/2156759X0801100503, 2018, 33.

[16]Education Trust. "Closing the Achievement Gap, 2005, Retrieved March 1, 2009, from http://www2.edtrust.org/edtrust.

CHAPTER TWO
WHAT WILL EDUCATORS DO WITH THIS TRUTH?

[1]R. J. Skiba, R. S. Michael, A. C. Nardo, and R. Peterson "The Color of Discipline: Sources of Racial and Gender Disproportionality in School Punishment (Lincoln: University of Nebraska [Policy Research Report #SRS1], 2000).

[2]Advancement Project/Civil Rights Project, "Education Denied: The Negative Impact of Zero Tolerance Policies," Washington, D. C.: Testimony before the United States Commission on Civil Rights, 2000; P. Allen-Meares, "African American Males: Their Status, Educational Plight and the Possibilities for Their Future, 1999, as cited in L. Davis (Ed.), "Working with African American Males: A Guide to Practice," Thousand Oaks, Calif: Sage Publications, pp. 117-128; Courtland C. Lee, "Empowering Young Black Males," Ann Arbor: ERIC Clearinghouse on Counseling and Personnel Services, 1996; J. Trescott, "Fate, Hope and the Black Child," *Emerge*, 1990, 1(7), pp. 22-26.

[3]Donna Y. Ford, T. C. Grantham, and D. F. Bailey, "Identifying Giftedness Among African American Males: Recom-

mendations for Effective Recruitment and Retention," 1999, as cited in V. C. Polite and J. E. Davis (Eds), "African American Males in School and Society: Practices and Policies for Effective Education" (New York: Teachers College Press.; J. Trescott, "Fate, Hope and the Black Child," 51-67.

[4]Trescott, "Fate, Hope and the Black Child."

[5]U.S. Census Bureau, "Educational Attainment in the United States: 1998 Population Statistics," Washington, D.C.: U.S. Department of Commerce, June 1998.

[6]Orfield, Gary. 2001. "Schools More Separate: Consequences of a Decade of Resegregation," Cambridge, Mass.: The Civil Rights Project, Harvard University, 2001.

[7]Jerome H. Skolnick and Elliott Currie, *Crisis in American Institutions,* 9th ed., New York: HarperCollins, 1994.

[8]National Research Council, "A Common Destiny: Blacks and American Society. Washington, DC: National Academy Press, 1989; Alvin F. Poussaint and Amy Alexander, *Lay My Burden Down: Unraveling Suicide and the Mental Health Crisis Among African Americans*, Boston: Beacon Press, 2001.

[9]James A. Auerbach, Barbara K. Krimgold and Bonnie Lefkowitz, "Improving Health: It Doesn't Take a Revolution," Monograph on Health and Social Inequality, Washington, DC: Kellogg Foundation, 2000; Centers for Disease Control, "Distribution of AIDS Cases by Racial/ethnic Group and Exposure Category: United States from June 1, 1981 to July 4, 1988, *Morbidity and Mortality Weekly Report*, 1988, 55, 1-10; Howard B. Kaplan, Robert J. Johnson, Carol A. Bailey, and William Simon, "The Sociological Study of AIDS: A Critical Review

of the Literature and Suggested Research Agenda," *Journal of Health and Social Science Behavior*, 1987, 28, 140-157.

[10] Jewelle Taylor Gibbs, Ed., *Young, Black and Male in America: An Endangered Species*, Santa Barbara: Auburn House Publishing, 1988; Bruce R. Hare, "Structural Inequality and the Endangered Status of Black Youth, *Journal of Negro Education*, 1987, 56 (1), 100-110; Bruce R. Hare and L. A. Castenell, "No Place to Run, No Place to Hide: Comparative Status and Future Prospects of Black Boys, 1985.

[11]Iris Marion Young, *Inclusion and Democracy*, Oxford: Oxford University Presss, 2000, p. 97.

[12]James Coleman, Ernest Q. Campbell, Carol J. Hobson, James McPartland, Alexander M. Mood, Frederick D. Weinfield, and Robert L. York, "Equality of Educational Opportunity," Washington, D.C.: Government Printing Office, 1966.

[13]Donna Y. Ford and J. J. Harris, "On Discovering the Hidden Treasures of Gifted and Talented Black Children," *Roeper Review*, 1993, 13, 27-32; Jawanza Kunjufu, *Countering the Conspiracy to Destroy Black Boys*, Vol. 2, Chicago: African American Images, 1986.

[14]Karl L. Alexander, and Doris R. Entwhistle, "Achievement in the First Two Years of School: Patterns and Processes," Monographs of the Society for Research in Child Development, Johns Hopkins University, 1988, 53 (2), 157.

[15]John U. Ogbu, *Minority Education and Caste: The American System in Cross-Cultural Perspective*, New York: McGraw-Hill, 1978.

[16]K. C. Booker, "Likeness, Comfort, and Tolerance: Exam-

ining African American Adolescents' Sense of School Belonging," *The Urban Review*, 2007, 39(3), 301-317.

[17]*Ibid.*

[18]Jeremy D. Finn, "Withdrawing from School," *Review of Educational Research*, 1989, 59, 117-142.; Carol Goodenow, "Strengthening the Links Between Educational Psychology and the Study of Social Context." *Educational Psychologist*, 1992, 27, 177-196, 10.1207/s15326985ep2702_4; Karen F. Osterman, "Students' Need for Belonging in the School Community," *Review of Educational Research*, 2000, 70, 323-367.

[19]R. F. Baumeister and M. R. Leary, "The Need to Belong: Desire for Interpesonal Attachments as Fundamental Human Motivation," *Psychology Bulletin*, 1995 May; 117(3):497-529; Heather M. Chipuer, "Dyadic Attachments and Community Connectedness: Links with Youths' Loneliness Experiences," *Journal of Community Psychology*, 2001, 29, 1-18.

[20]Lisa Peterson and Jan Hughes, "The Differences Between Retained and Promoted Children in Educational Services Received," *Psychol Schol*, 2011, Feb. 1; 48(2) 156-165, retrieved from https://www.ncbi.nlm.nih.gov/pmc/articles/PMC3039171/.

[21]*Ibid.*

[22]*Ibid.*

[23]*Ibid.*

[24]Ashley Green, "14-Year Study: Holding Students Back in Grade School Hurts Their Chances of Graduating, March 27, 2018, *Texas A&M Today*, https://today.tamu.edu/2018/03/27/14-year-study-holding-students-back-in-grade-school-hurts-their-chances-of-graduating, accessed October 1, 2019.

[25]Donna Y. Ford and J. John Harris Russo, III, "On Discovering the Hidden Treasures of Gifted and Talented Black Children," *Roeper Review*, 1993, 13, 27-32.

[26]Valerie O. Pang and V. A. Sablan, "Teacher Efficacy: How Do Teachers Feel About Their Abilities to Teach African-American Students?" 1998, as cited in Mary E. Dilworth, Ed., "Being Responsive to Cultural Differences: How Teachers Learn," Washington, D.C., American Association of Colleges for Teacher Education, 1998, 39-58.

[27]John Ogbu, "Cultural Diversity and Human Development," as cited in D. T. Slaughter, "Black Children and Poverty: A Developmental Perspective," San Francisco: Jossey-Bass, 1998, 11-28; James P. Connell, Margaret B. Spencer and J. Lawrence Aber, "Educational Risk and Resilience in African-American Youth: Context, Self and Action Outcomes in School" *Child Development*, 1994, 65, 493–506.

[28]W. B. Brookover and E. L. Erickson, *Society, Schools, and Learning*, Boston: Allyn and Bacon, 1969; Raymond A. Morrow and Carlos A. Torres, *Social Theory and Education: A Critique of Theories of Social and Cultural Reproduction*, Albany: SUNY Press, 1995.

[29]U.S. Department of Education, "U.S. Department of Education Releases 2015-16 Civil Rights Data Collection," April 24, 2018, https://www.ed.gov/news/press-releases/us-department-education-releases-2015-16-civil-rights-data-collection, accessed October 1, 2019.

[30]*Ibid.*

[31]U.S. Department of Education, "Civil Rights Data Col-

lection (CRDC), 2018, https://www2.ed.gov/about/offices/list/ocr/data.html, accessed October 1, 2019.

[32]Sarah D. Sparks and Alyson Klein, "Discipline Disparities Grow for Students of Color, New Federal Data Show," April 24, 2018, *Education Week,* https://www.edweek.org/ew/articles/2018/04/24/discipline-disparities-grow-for-students-of-color.html?cmp=soc-twitter-shr, accessed October1, 2019.

[33]Kirsten Weir, "Inequality at School: What's Behind the Racial Disparity in Our Education System?" *American Psychological Association*, November 2016, Vol. 47, No. 10.

[34]Civil Rights Data Collection, "Data Snapshot: School Discipline, Issue Brief No. 1 (March 2014), https://ocrdata.ed.gov/Downloads/CRDC-School-Discipline-Snapshot.pdf, accessed October 1, 2019.

[35]Kunjufu, *Countering the Conspiracy to Destroy Black Boys,* Vol. 2, 21.

[36]Brookover and Erickson, "Society, Schools and Learning"; Morrow and Torres, *Social Theory and Education.*

[37]John M. Wallace, Jr., Ph.D., Sara Goodkind, Ph.D., Cynthia M. Wallace and Jerald G. Bachman, "Racial, Ethnic, and Gender Differences in School Discipline among U.S. High School Students: 1991-2005," National Institute of Health, https://www.ncbi.nlm.nih.gov/pmc/articles/PMC2678799/, accessed October 1, 2019.

[38]Pedro A. Noguera, The Trouble with Black Boys: The Role and Influence of Environmental and Cultural Factors on the Academic Performance of African American Males, Harvard Journal of African American Public Policy, 2001, 2, 23-46., 17.

[39]Richard Majors and Janet M. Billson, *Cool Pose: Dilemmas*

of Black Manhood in America, New York: Simon & Schuster Publishing Co., 4.

[40]Gibbs, *Young, Black and Male in America*; Jacqueline J. Irvine, *Black Students and School Failure: Policies, Practices and Prescriptions*, New York: Greenwood Press, 1990; Vernon C. Polite and James E. Davis, Eds., "African-American Males in School and Society: Policy and Practice for Effective Education," New York: Teachers College Press, 1999.

[41]Majors & Billson, *Cool Pose*; Noguera, "The Trouble with Black Boys."

[42]Dee Norman Lloyd, "Prediction of School Failure from Third-Grade Data, *Educational and Psychological Measurement*, 1978, 38, 1193-1200, https://doi.org/10.1177/001316447803800442.

[43]Robert D. Hoge and Laurinda Cudmore, "The Use of Teacher-Judgment Measures in the Identification of Gifted Pupils," *Teaching and Teacher Education*, 1986, 2, 181-196.

[44]M. Suzanne Donovan and Christopher T. Cross, Eds., "Minority Students in Special and Gifted Education, Washington, DC: National Academy Press, 2002, 80.

[45]Matthew McBee, "A Descriptive Analysis of Referral Sources for Gifted Identification Screening by Race and Socioeconomic Status," 2006, *Journal of Advanced Academics*, 17, 103-111. 10.4219/jsge-2006-686.

[46]Hala Elhoweris, Kagendo Mutua, Negmeldin Alseikh, and Pauline Holloway, "Effect of Children's Ethnicity on Teachers' Referral and Recommendation Decisions in Gifted and Talented Programs," 2005, https://doi.org/10.1177/07419325 050260010401; Ronald Ferguson, "Teachers' Perceptions and

Expectations and the Black-White Test Score Gap," 2003, *Urban Education*, 38, 10.1177/0042085903038004006; Matthew McBee, "A Descriptive Analysis of Referral Sources for Gifted Identification Screening by Race and Socioeconomic Status"; S. B. Woods and V. H. Achy, *Yes, We Can: Telling Truths and Dispelling Myths about Race and Education in America*, Washington, D.C.: The Education Trust, 2006.

[47]Morris Rosenberg, *Conceiving the Self*, New York: Basic Books, 1979; Abraham Tesser, "Toward a Self-Evaluation Maintenance Model of Social Behavior," 1988, 10.1016/S0065-2601(08)60227-0.

[48]M. Monique McMillian-Robinson, Henry T. Frierson and Frances A. Campbell, "Do Gender Differences Exist in the Academic Identification of African-American Elementary-School Aged Children?" National Institute of Health, https://www.ncbi.nlm.nih.gov/pmc/articles/PMC4002045/, accessed October 1, 2019.

[49]Jennifer Crocker and Brenda Major, "Social Stigma and Self-Esteem: The Self-Protective Properties of Stigma," 1989, *Psychological Review*, 96, 4, 608-630; Brenda Major and Toni Schmader, T. "Coping with Stigma Through Psychological Disengagement, 1998, American Psychological Association, https://psycnet.apa.org/record/1998-07621-010; Shelley E. Taylor and Jonathon D. Brown, "Illusion and Well-being: A Social-Psychological Perspective on Mental Health, 1988, *Psychological Bulletin*, 103, 193-210; Tesser, "Toward a Self-Evaluation Maintenance Model of Social Behavior; Abraham Tesser and Jennifer Campbell, "Self-definition: The Impact of

the Relative Performance and Similarity of Others, 1980, *Social Psychology Quarterly*, 43, 341-347.

[50]Majors and Billson, *Cool Pose*; John U. Ogbu, "Understanding Cultural Diversity and Learning, 1992, *Educational Researcher*, 27(8), 4-14; Claude M. Steele, "A Threat in the Air: How Stereotypes Shape Intellectual Identity and Performance, 1997, *American Psychologist*, 52, 613–629.

[51]Patricia Phelan, Ann Locke Davidson and Hanh Thanh Cao, "Students' Multiple Worlds: Negotiating the Boundaries of Family, Peer, and School Cultures," 1998, *Anthropology and Education Quarterly*, 22, 224-250.

[52]Diane Ravitch, *Left Back: A Century of Failed School Reforms,* New York: Simon & Schuster, 2000; Marc S. Tucker and Judy B. Codding, *Standards for Our Schools: How to Set Them, Measure Them and Reach Them,* San Francisco: Jossey-Bass, 1998.

[53]Kunjufu, *Countering the Conspiracy to Destroy Black Boys*; Haki R. Madhubuti, *Black Men: Obsolete, Single, Dangerous? The Afrikan American Family in Transition [Essays in Discovery, Solution, and Hope],* Chicago: Third World Press, 1990; Majors and Billson, *Cool Pose*; Cornel West, *Race Matters,* Boston: Beacon Press, 1993.

[54]Claude M. Steele and Joshua Aronson, "Stereotype Threat and the Intellectual Test Performance of African-Americans, 1995, *Journal of Personality and Social Psychology*, 69, 797-811.

[55]Michele Foster, *Black Teachers on Teaching*, New York: The New Press, 1997; Ladson-Billings, *The Dreamkeepers: Successful Teachers of African American Children,* 2nd Ed., San

Francisco: Josse-Bass Publishers, 2009; Carol D. Lee, "The State of Knowledge About the Education of African Americans, Washington, DC: American Educational Research Association, Commission on Black Education, 2000.

[56]Prudence L. Carter, "Race and Cultural Flexibility Among Students in Different Multiracial Schools," 2005, Teachers College Record, 112. 1529-1574.

[57]C. Lee, "Unpacking Culture, Teaching, and Learning: A Response to the Pedagogy of Power, 2001, cited in William Watkins, James H. Lewis and Victoria Chou (Eds.), *Race and Education: The Roles of History and Society in Educating African-American Students,* Boston: Allyn Bacon, 2000, 89-99; Angela Valenzuela, *Subtractive Schooling: U.S.-Mexican Youth and the Politics of Caring.* Albany: State University of New York Press, 1999.

[58]Steele, "A Threat in the Air"; Majors and Billson, *Cool Pose.*

CHAPTER FOUR
MEET "ISLAND 9"

[1]AVID is an acronym for **A**dvancement **V**ia **I**ndividual **D**etermination, a program designed to help underachieving students with high academic potential prepare for entrance to colleges and universities.

[2]The California High School Exit Examination.

[3]Nel Noddings, "Care and Coercion in School Reform," 2001, *Journal of Educational Change,*" 2:35. https://doi.org/10.1023/A:101151 4928048; Gloria Ladson-Billings, Ed.,

Critical Race Theory Perspectives on the Social Studies: The Profession, Policies, and Curriculum, Greenwich, Conn.: Information Age Publishing, 2003;
Gloria Ladson-Billings, "Yes, But How Do We Do It? Practicing Culturally Relevant Pedagogy, 2006, ESED 5234—Master List. 37,https://digitalcommons.georgiasouthern.edu/esed5234-master/37.

⁴Angela Love and Ann C. Kruger, 2005, "Teacher Beliefs and Student Achievement in Urban Schools Serving African American Students," 2005, *Journal of Educational Research,* J EDUC RES. 99. 87-98. 10.3200/JOER.99.2.87-98; Ladson-Billings, *The Dreamkeepers.*

⁵Ladson-Billings, *The Dreamkeepers.*

⁶Nel Noddings, "Care and Coercion in School Reform," 2001, Journal of Educational Change, 2: 35. https://doi.org/10.1023/A:1011514928048.

⁷Bronwyn E. Becker and Suniya S. Luthar, "Prvileged but Pressured? A Study of Affluent Youth, Society for Research in Child Development, https://doi.org/10.1111/1467-8624.00492, 2003; John Dewey, *Experience and Nature.* New York: Dover Publications, 1958; Jennifer R. C. Fredricks, Phyllis Blumenfeld, and Allison H. Paris, "School Engagement: Potential of the Concept, State of the Evidence," *Sage Journals,* https://doi.org/10.3102/00346543074001059, 2004; Karen F. Osterman, "Students' Need for Belonging in the School Community, 2000, *Review of Educational Research,* https://doi.org/10.3102/00346543070003323, 70, 323-367.

⁸James P. Connell and James G. Wellborn, "Competence,

Autonomy and Relatedness: A Motivational Analysis of Self-Esteem Processes," 1991, cited in M. Gunnar and A. Sroufe, Eds., Minnesota Symposium on Child Psychology, 43-77.

[9]Ladson-Billings, *The Dreamkeepers*; Gloria Ladson-Billings and Annette Henry, *"Blurring the Borders: Voices of African Liberatory Pedagogy in the United States and Canada,"* Vol. 172, Iss. 2, 1990, 72-88; Theresa Perry and Lisa Delpit, *The Real Ebonics Debate: Power, Language and the Education of African-American Children,* Boston: Beacon Press, 1998.

[10]Gloria Ladson-Billings, *The Dreamkeepers.*

[11]TABSE, 2019

[12]Osterman, "Students' Need for Belonging in the School Community."

[13]Urie Bronfenbrenner, *The Ecology of Human Development*, Cambridge: Harvard University Press, 1979.

[14]Dena Phillips Swanson, Michael Cunningham, Margaret B. Spencer, "Black Males' Structural Conditions Achievement Patterns, Normative Needs, and 'Opportunities,'" 2003, Urban Education, 38, 608-633.

[15]Carol Goodenow, "The Psychological Sense of School Membership Among Adolescents: Scale Development and Educational Correlates, 1993, *Psychology in the Schools*, 30, 79-90.

[16]Majors and Billson, *Cool Pose*; Steele, "A Threat in the Air," *American Psychologist*, 52, 613–629.

[17]Theresa Perry, "Toward a Theory of African American School Achievement (Report No. 16). Baltimore: Center on Families, Communities, Schools and Children's Learning, 1993; Margaret Beale Spencer, Elizabeth Noll, Jill Stoltzful and

Vinay Harpalani, (2001). "Identity and School Adjustment: Revisiting the 'Acting White' Assumption, 2001 *Educational Psychologist*, 36, 21-30; Meyer Weinberg, *A Chance to Learn: A History of Race and Education in the United States*, Cambridge: Cambridge University Press, 1977.

[18]Ladson-Billings, "Culturally Responsive Teaching"; Perry and Delpit, "The Real Ebonics Debate."

[19]Lynley H. Anderman, "Academic and Social Perceptions as Predictors of Change in Middle School Students' Sense of School Belonging, 2003, *The Journal of Experimental Education*, 72, 5-22.; Connell and Wellborn, "Competence, Autonomy and Relatedness."

[20]Researchers use triangulation for four primary reasons: 1) enriching, adding value to by explaining different aspects of an issue; 2) refuting, a hypothesis generation by a set of options is disproved; 3) confirming, one set of options confirms a hypothesis generated by another set of options; 3) explaining, one set of options sheds light on unexpected findings derived from another set of options [Soniya Carvalho and Howard White, "Combining the Quantitative and Qualitative Approaches to Poverty Measurement and Analysis: The Practice and the Potential." World Bank Technical Paper 366. Washington, D.C.: World Bank, 1997].